# Woodstock Ontario Book 4 in Colour Photos, Saving Our History One Photo at a Time

Photography
by Barbara Raué
©2019

Series Name: Cruising Ontario

Book 244: Woodstock Book 4

Cover photo: 81 Light Street, Page 9

©All the photos in this book have been taken with my cameras. I own the rights to them.

Series Name: Cruising Ontario, Saving Our History One Photo at a Time in colour photos

Books Available in Alphabetical Order:
Aberfoyle, Acton, Ajax, Alton, Amherstburg, Ancaster, Arthur, Auburn, Aylmer, Ayr, Beaver Valley, Belfountain, Belgrave, Belleville, Bloomingdale, Blyth, Brantford, Brockville, Burford, Burgessville, Burlington, Caledon, Caledonia, Cambridge, Carlow, Cayuga, Chatsworth, Cheltenham, Clifford, Colborne, Collingwood, Conestogo, Delhi, Dorchester to Aylmer, Drayton, Drumbo, Dundas, Dunlop, Dunnville, Eden Mills, Elmira, Elora, Embro, Erin, Essex, Fergus, Fort Erie, Georgetown, Goderich, Grimsby, Guelph, Hagersville, Haldimand County, Hamilton, Hanover, Harriston, Hespeler, Ingersoll, Inglewood, Innerkip, Jarvis, Kingston, Kingsville, Kitchener, Lake Superior, Lincoln, Linwood, Listowel, London, Lucknow, Merrickville, Mono, Mount Brydges, Mount Forest, Mount Pleasant, Neustadt, New Hamburg, Newboro, Newport, Niagara-on-the-Lake, Niagara Falls, North Bay, Norwich, Oakville, Onondaga, Orangeville, Orillia, Oshawa, Otterville, Owen Sound, Palmerston, Paris, Parry Sound, Pelham, Perth, Peterborough, Petrolia, Pickering, Port Colborne, Port Elgin, Port Hope, Port Perry, Portland, Preston, Rockwood, Sarnia, Sault Ste. Marie, Seaforth, Sheffield, Shelburne, Simcoe, Smiths Falls, Smithville, Southampton, Southwest Oxford, St. Catharines, St. George, St. Jacobs, St. Marys, St. Thomas, Stoney Creek, Stouffville, Stratford, Strathroy, Sudbury, Tavistock, Terra Cotta, Thamesford, Thunder Bay, Tillsonburg, Toronto, Uxbridge, Waterdown, Waterford, Waterloo, Welland, Wellesley, West Flamborough, Westport, Whitby, Windsor, Wingham, Woodstock, York, Zorra

Book 125-127: Woodstock
Book 238-239: Ingersoll
Book 240: Zorra Township
Book 241: Southwest Oxford
Book 242: Otterville, Burgessville
Book 243: Norwich
Book 244: Woodstock Book 4

Table of Contents

| | |
|---|---|
| Light Street | Page 5 |
| Perry Street | Page 45 |
| Chapel Street | Page 48 |
| Simcoe Street | Page 49 |
| Hatch Street | Page 50 |
| Peel Street | Page 55 |
| Jack Poole Drive | Page 60 |
| Architectural Terms | Page 61 |
| Building Styles | Page 62 |

Woodstock is located in the heart of South Western Ontario, at the junction of highways 401 and 403, 50 kilometers east of London and 60 kilometers west of Kitchener. Woodstock is the largest municipality in Oxford County.

Light Street memorializes A. W. Light, the first of the military officers to arrive in the area. He was a retired colonel, had published several books, and had many ideas and much enthusiasm for the settlement at the west end.

In the 1830s, British naval and army officers placed on half-pay were encouraged to settle in Oxford to ensure this community's loyalty to the British crown. The first to arrive was Alexander Whalley Light, a retired colonel who came to Oxford County in 1831. He was joined by Philip Graham in 1832, a retired captain of the Royal Navy, and Captain Andrew Drew, on half-pay from the Royal Navy, arrived in Woodstock to make preparations for his superior, Rear-Admiral Henry Vansittart, also on half-pay. Half-pay officers went to considerable lengths to clear their chosen parcels of land.

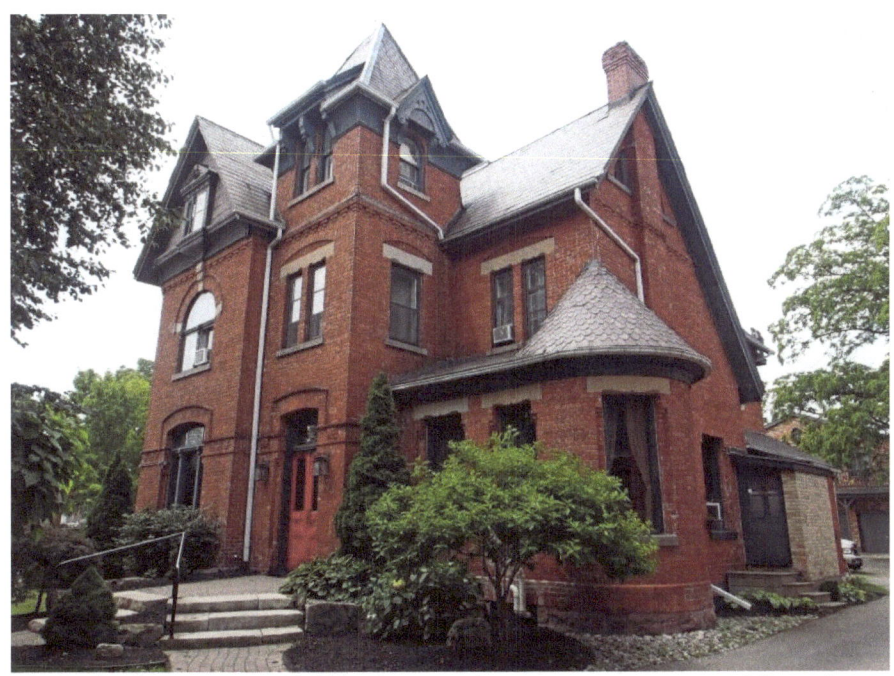

33 Light Street – c. 1869 - Queen Anne - two story with attic, red brick, slate roof with fish scale slate on towers, gable roof, styled stone lintel, keystone and drip course above windows and doorways, corbel cornice encircle the house at the eaves, dormer casement window in gable has pediment lintel, paired windows in square tower and wall dormer, square tower has steep hip roof, circular tower has cone roof, double door topped with segmental transom

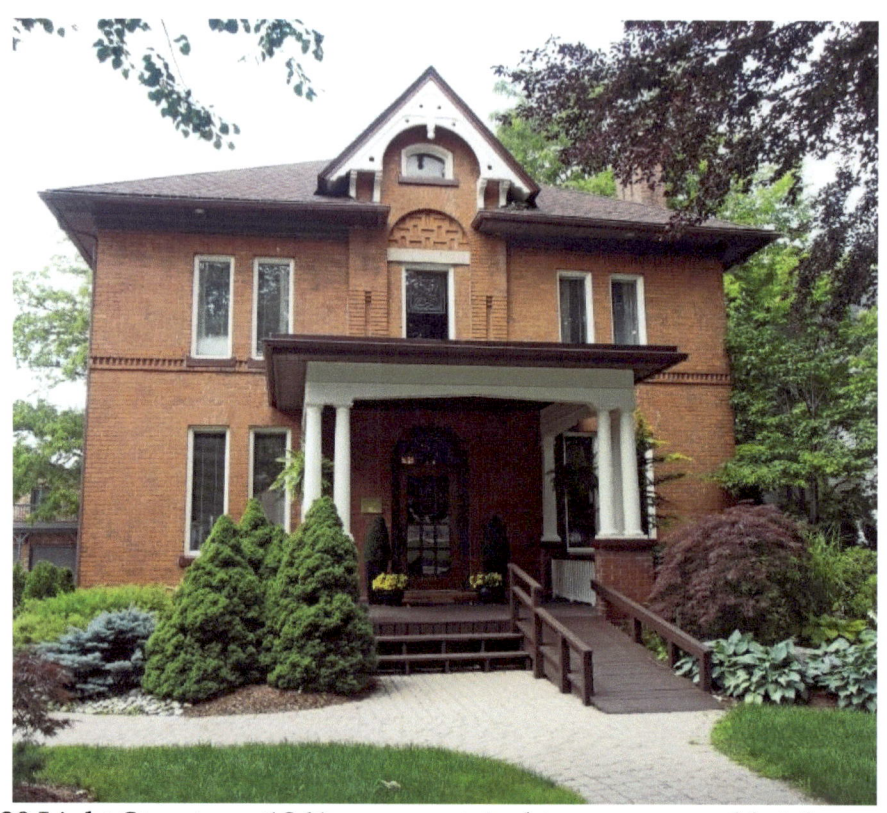

39 Light Street – c. 1861 - symmetrical two story, red brick, trunked hip roof, dormer with vergeboard and paired brackets, corbel bricking on chimneys, central window has stone lintel and basket weave bricks in semi-circle above window, soldier styled drip course, central door has ellipse shaped transom, paired Doric columns support open porch

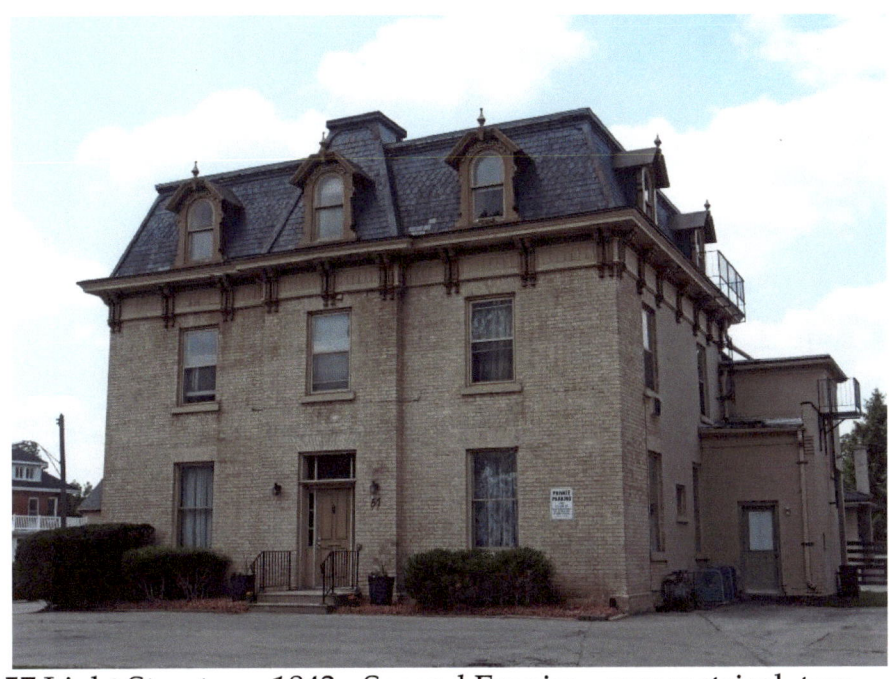

57 Light Street – c. 1843 - Second Empire - symmetrical, two story with attic, cleaned white brick, both regular and fish scale slate roof, dormers have decorative wood trim and finials, paired brackets, shutters, central door has sidelights and transom

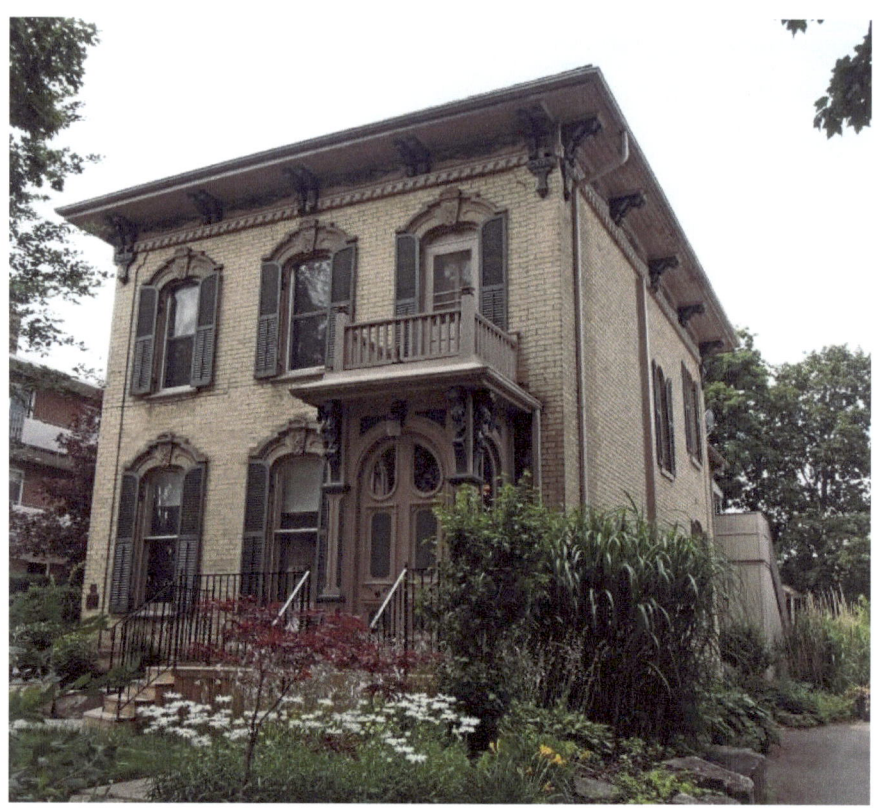

77 Light Street – 1878 - Italianate - two story, white brick, trunked hip roof, decorative cornice with dentil, paired brackets, cut stone lentils on windows, shutters, closed front porch has semi-circular heading, door has tear-drop windows, open balcony

James Hay established the Hay and Company in 1893, which specialized in plywood and veneer materials, later known as Weldwood. Active in Municipal affairs, he was Deputy Reeve and later Mayor 1893-1894. One of the early founders and directors of the Woodstock Board of Trade in 1877, he also built Woodstock's first waterworks to eliminate typhoid and provide fire protection. He was the first citizen in Woodstock to install telephones in his home and business in 1879.

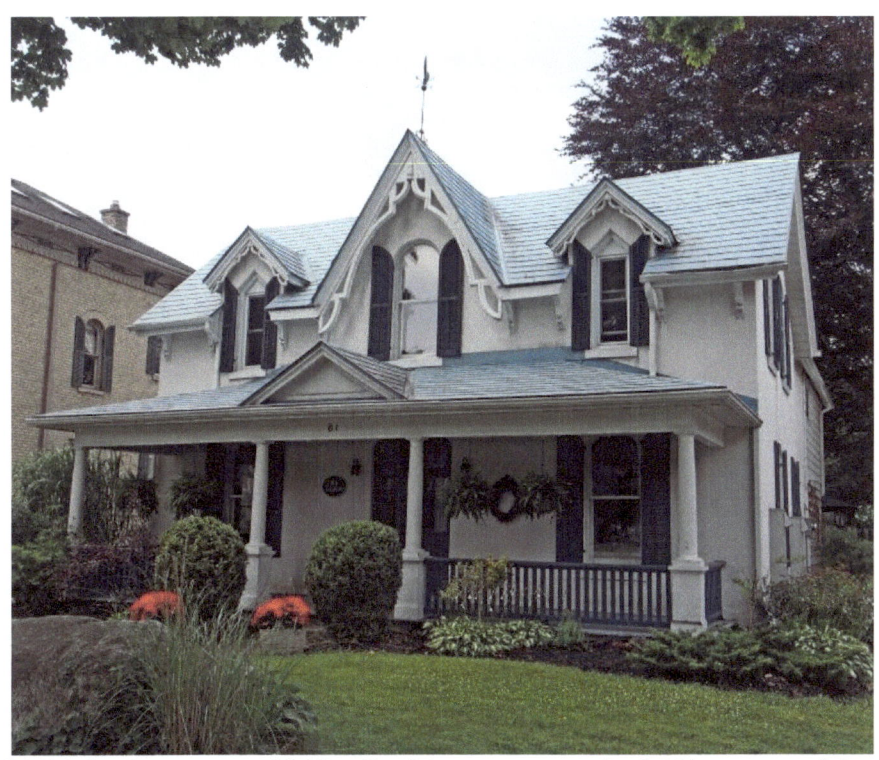

81 Light Street – c. 1849 - Gothic - symmetrical 1½ story, white stucco, gable roof, paired wall door and central gable have ribbon vergeboard, single brackets; one-over-one Gothic, flat and semi-circular windows, shutters; central paired front door, collared tapered Doric columns support pediment decorated open verandah

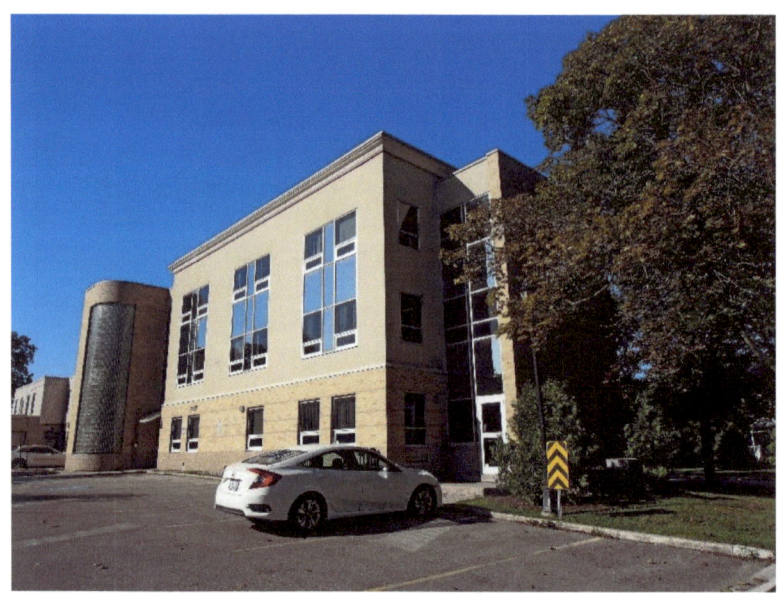

82 Light Street – Archives

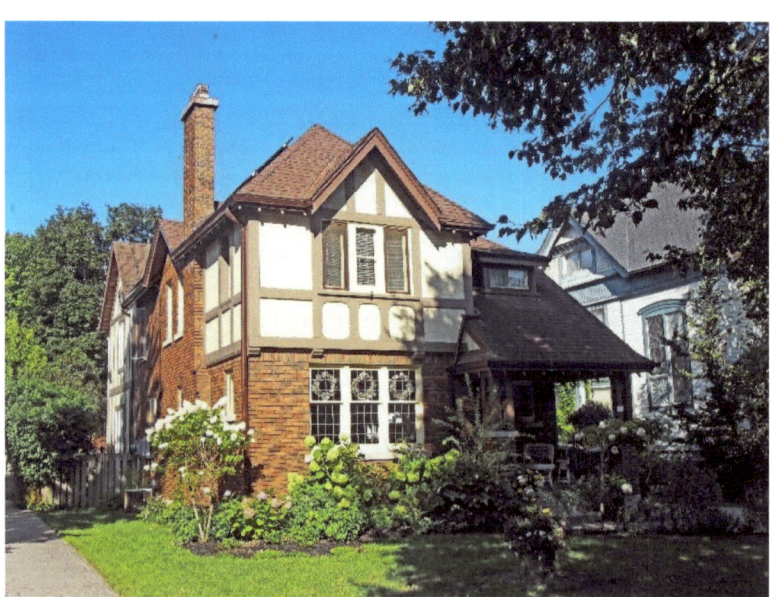

93 Light Street – c. 1849 - Modern Tudor architectural style – two-story, rug brick, trunked roof, shed dormer, off-centered door

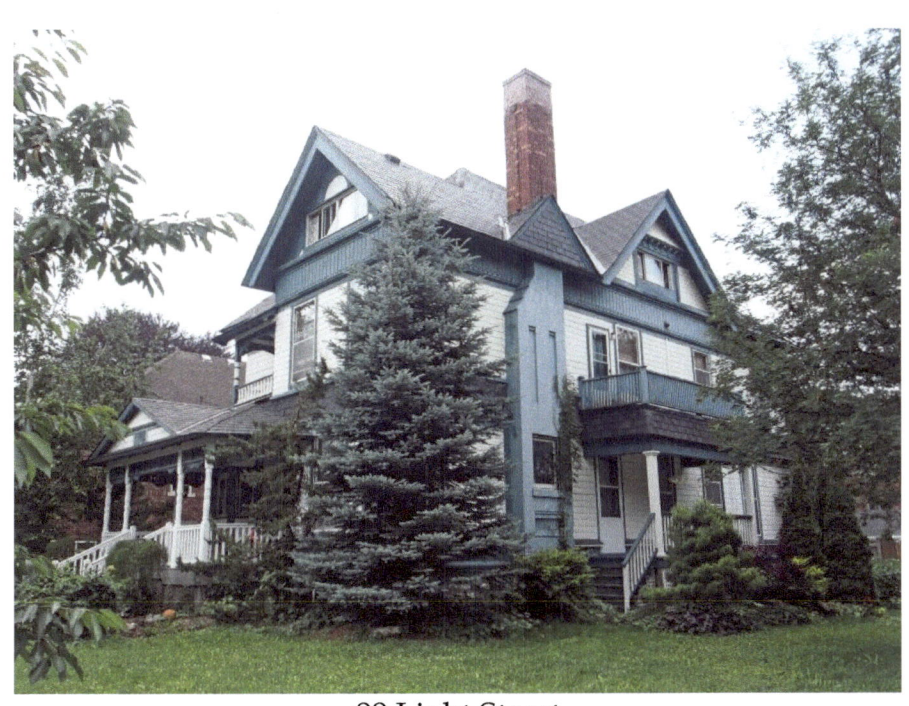

99 Light Street

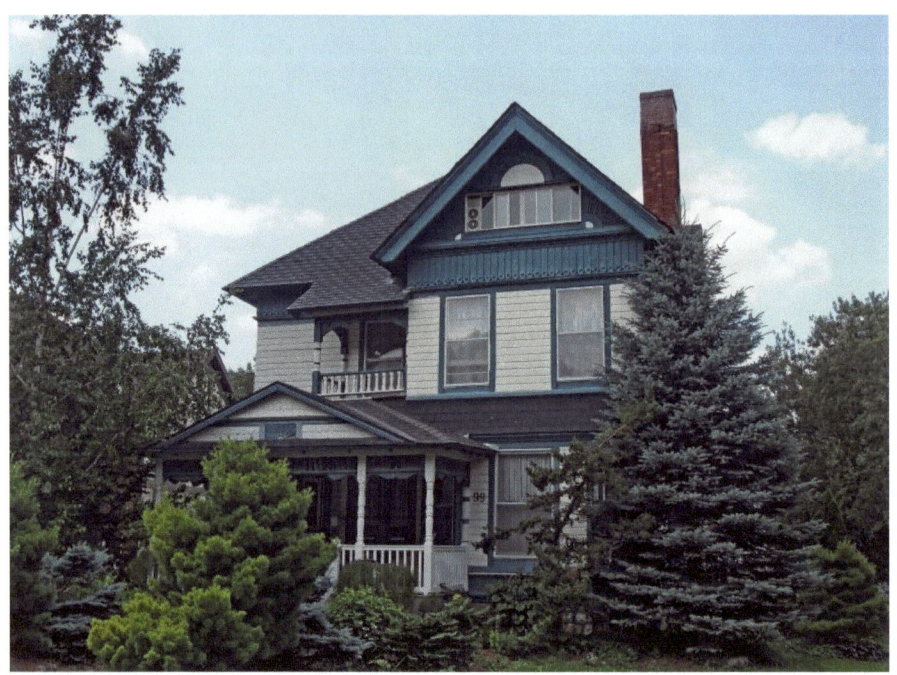

99 Light Street – c. 1849 - Queen Anne - two story with attic, wood clad, trunked hip roof with gables, stained glass window in stairwell with round, diamond painted and stained glass, stained glass between flues, colored posts, spindles and bric-a-brac decorate open verandahs, open balcony

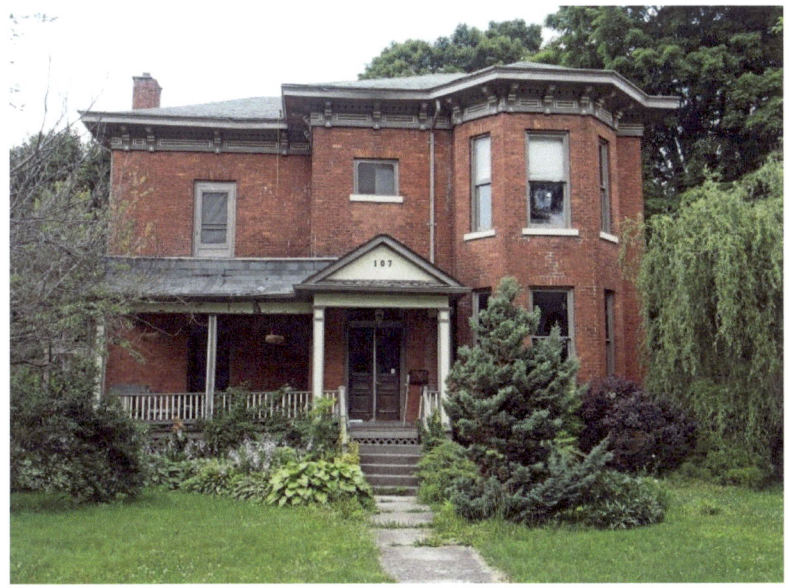

107 Light Street – c. 1882 - Italianate - two story, red brick, trunked hip roof, single brackets, two-story bay window, off-centered double doors, collared square posts support open verandah and open balcony

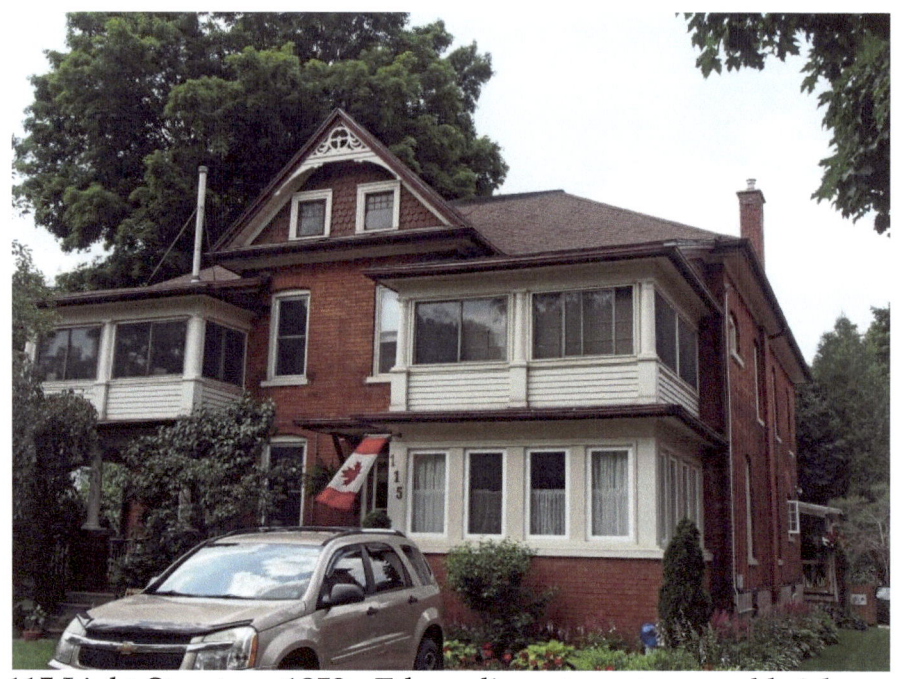

115 Light Street - c. 1853 - Edwardian - two story, red brick, semi-detached, trunked hip roof, gable with delicate vergeboard above entrances, large closed balconies, verandah open/closed

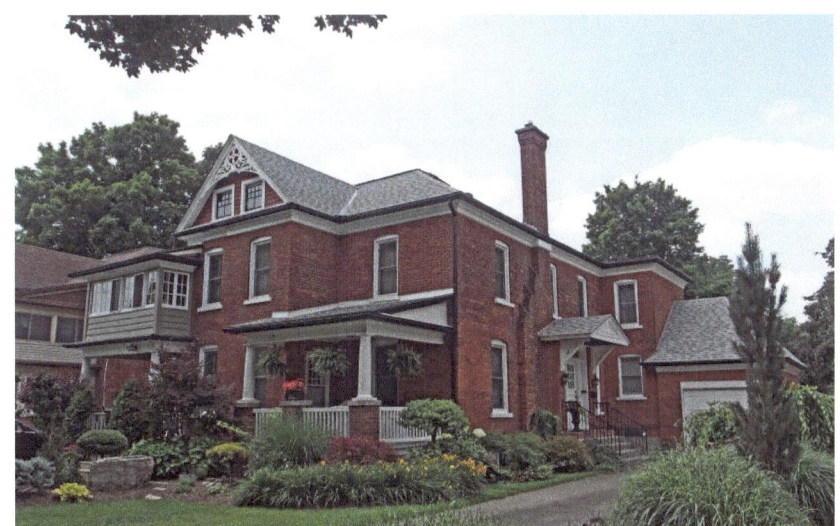

119 Light Street - c. 1865 - Edwardian - two story, red brick, semi-detached, trunked hip roof, gable with delicate vergeboard above entrances

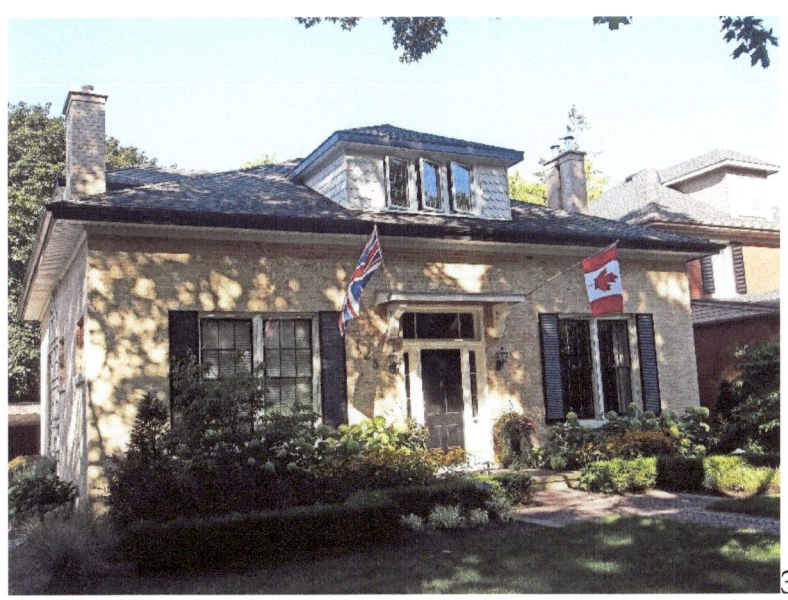

125 Light Street – c. 1861 - Edwardian style, one story with attic, painted brick, hip roof with dormers, centered door with sidelights and transom

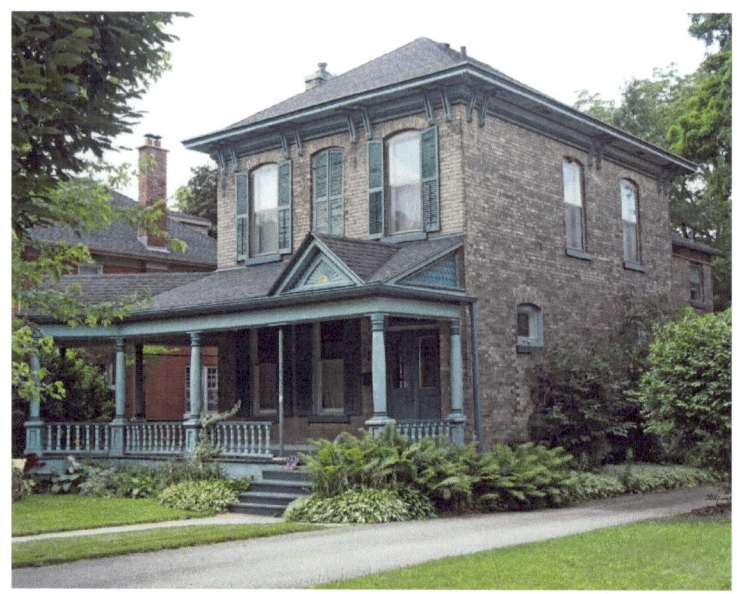

135 Light Street – Italianate, paired cornice brackets, segmented windows, double front doors, and uniquely-shaped verandah supported by Doric pillars; offset section of verandah allowed cooler air to circulate

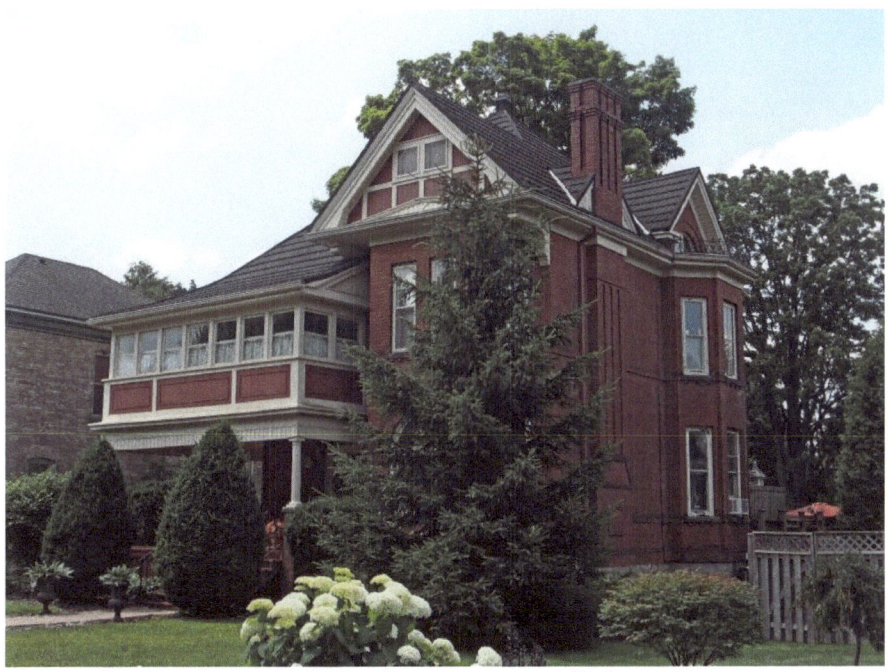

139 Light Street – c. 1875 - Queen Anne, Edwardian - two story with attic, red brick, hip roof with gable ends, first floor semi-circular stained-glass window, drip molding above curbed bricks below, tapered Doric columns support a large open verandah and closed balcony

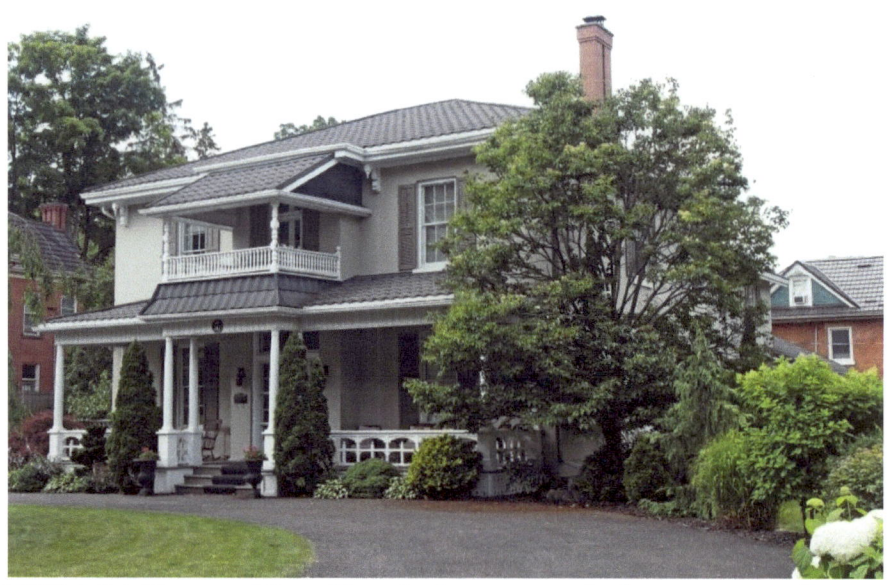

147 Light Street – Neo-Classical symmetrical two-storey home with painted brick; 6/6 double hung windows and decorative shutters; tapered Doric pillars support an open verandah and open balcony; sidelights and transom flank the centered entrance

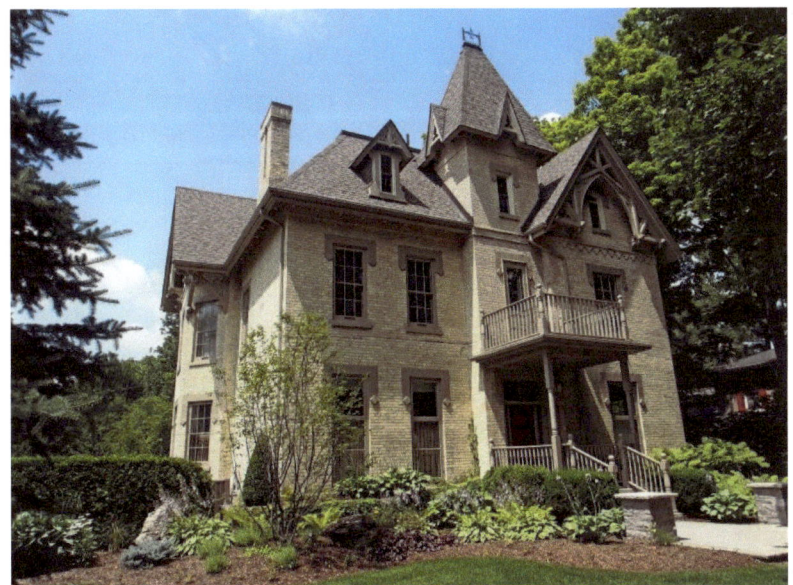

157 Light Street – built in 1875 – Queen Anne style with varied roof line, decorated verge board on gables, dormers and tower; second-floor balcony

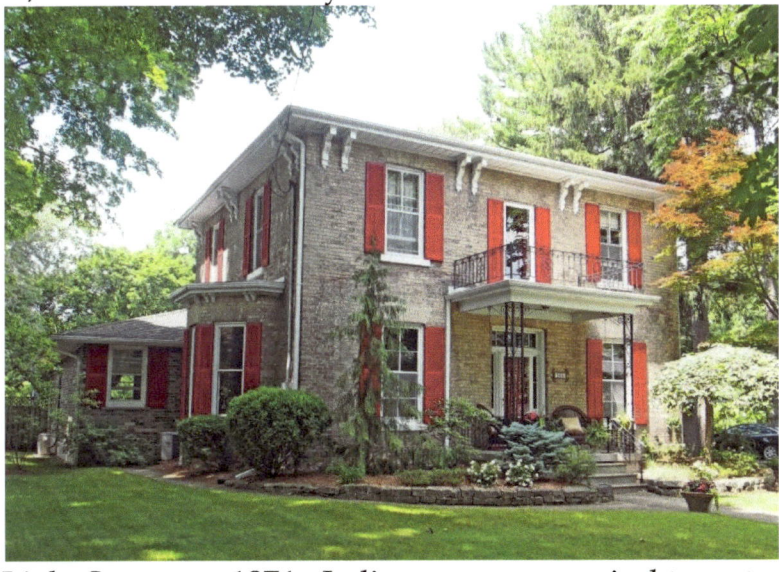

165 Light Street – c. 1874 - Italianate - symmetrical two story, white brick, hip roof, paired brackets equally distributed, side lights and transom flank centered door

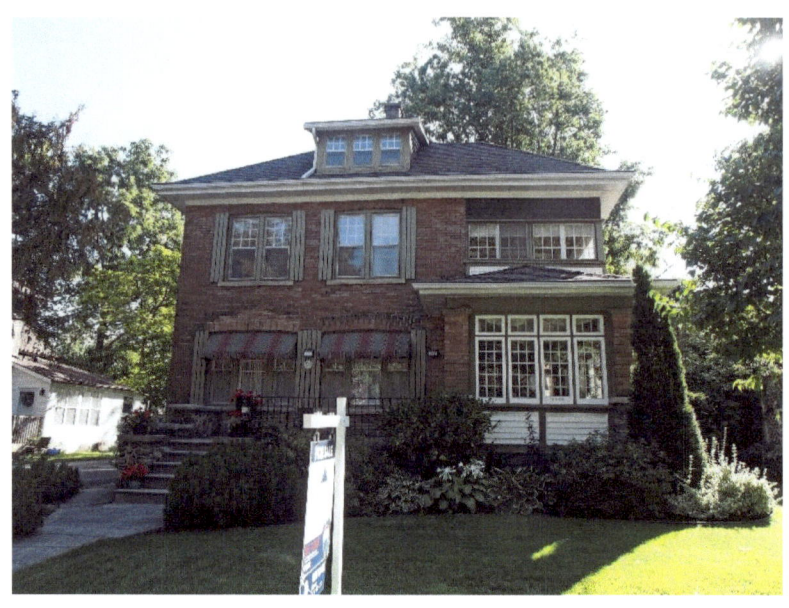

162 Light Street – c. 1862 – two story with attic, hip roof with shed dormers

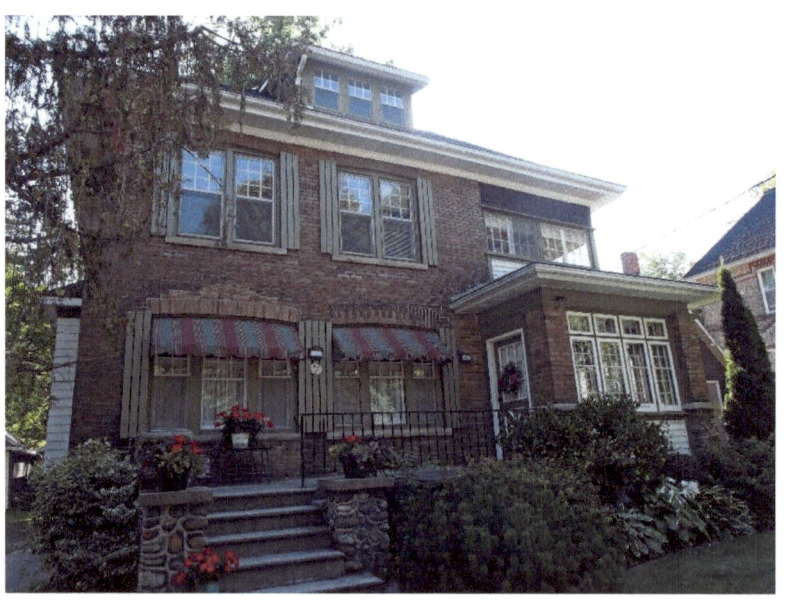

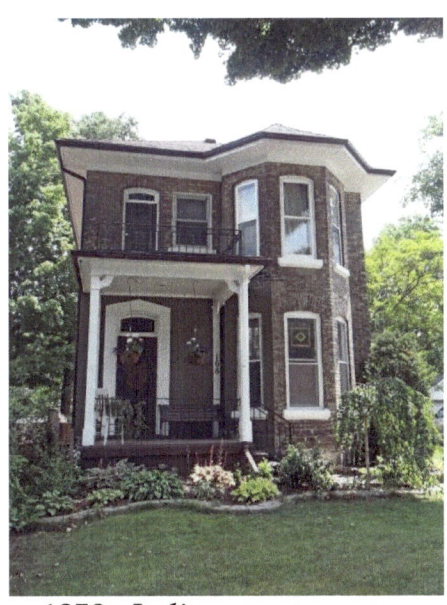

168 Light Street c. 1850 - Italianate - two story, white brick, hip roof, small brackets, two-story bay, off-centered door has segmental head transom

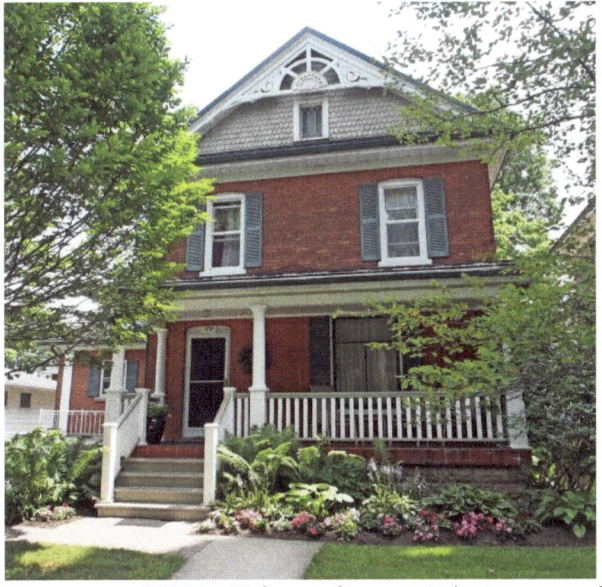

172 Light Street – c. 1877 - Edwardian – 1½ story, red brick, painted green shingles in gable end with sunburst vergeboard, gable roof, off-centered door with open verandah

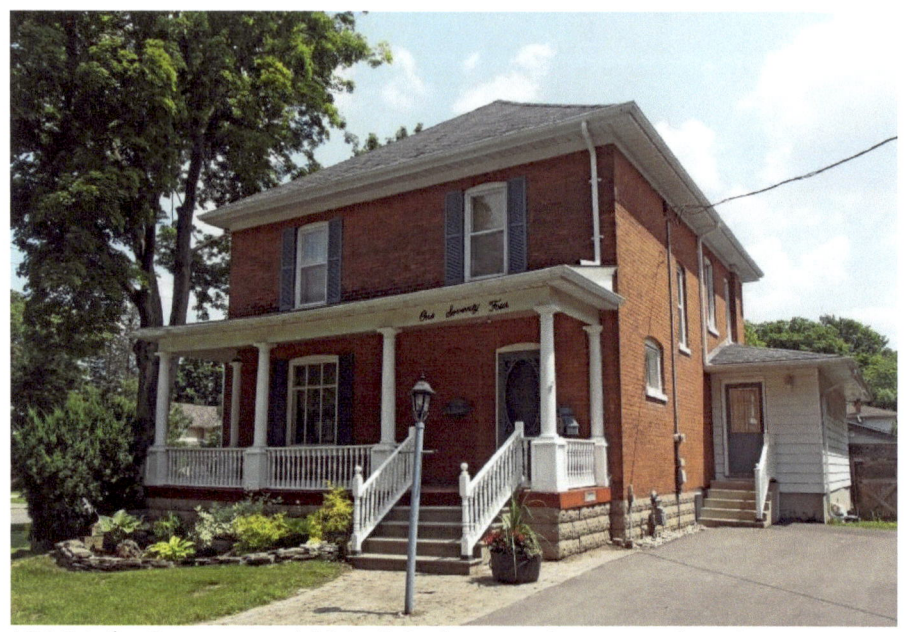

174 Light Street – c. 1886 - Modern architectural style - two story, rug brick, hip roof, four-over-one rectangular windows are in groups

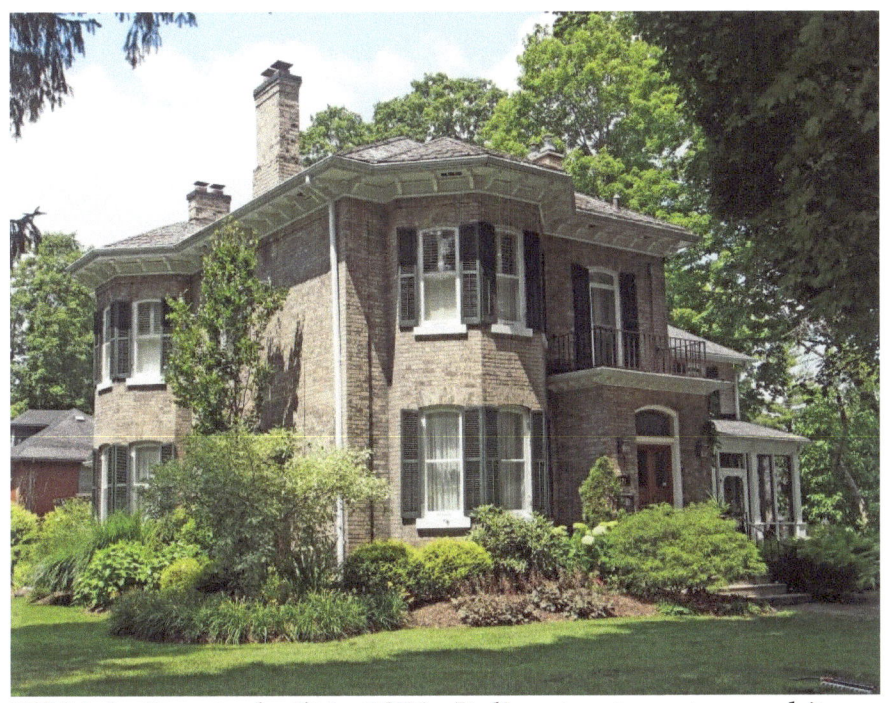

177 Light Street – built in 1876 - Italianate - two story, white brick, trunked hip roof, many small brackets, two-story bay, off-centered double doors, new segmental hand stained glass transom, shutters

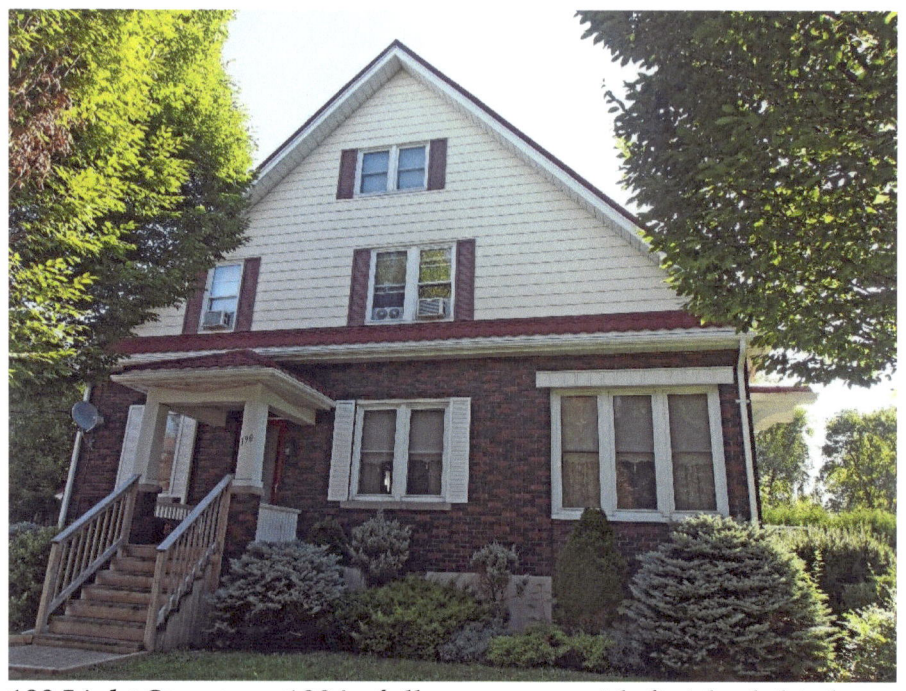

190 Light Street - c. 1906 - full two story with finished third floor, rug brick and soft yellow siding, double dwelling, porch supported by squared posts

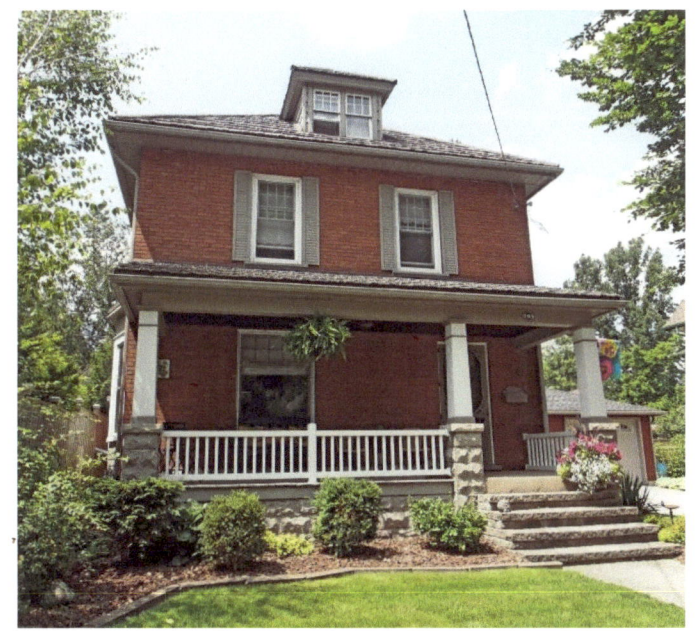

193 Light Street – Edwardian red brick two-storey home – open verandah with tapered Doric posts on large cement piers

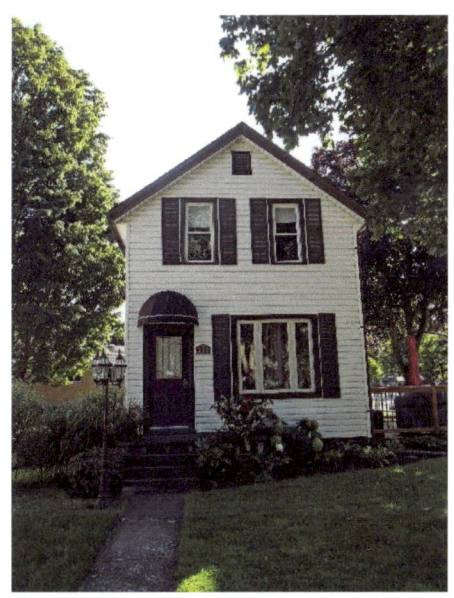

212 Light Street – Ontario Vernacular architectural style, 1½-story

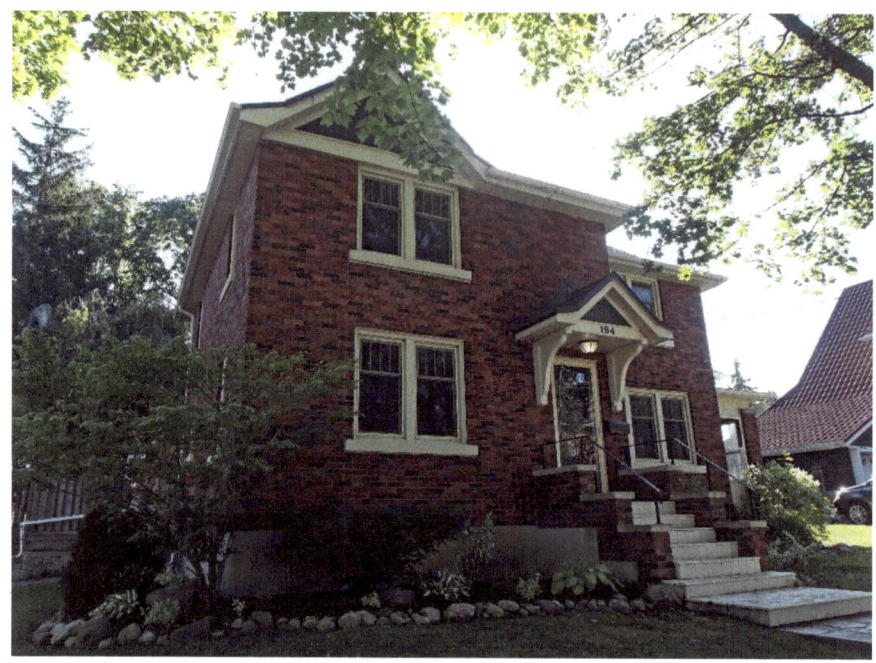

194 Light Street - c. 1910 - Modern architectural style, two story, rug brick, hip roof, four-over-one rectangular windows, gable roof porch hood supported by large decorative brackets, open porch with brick balusters

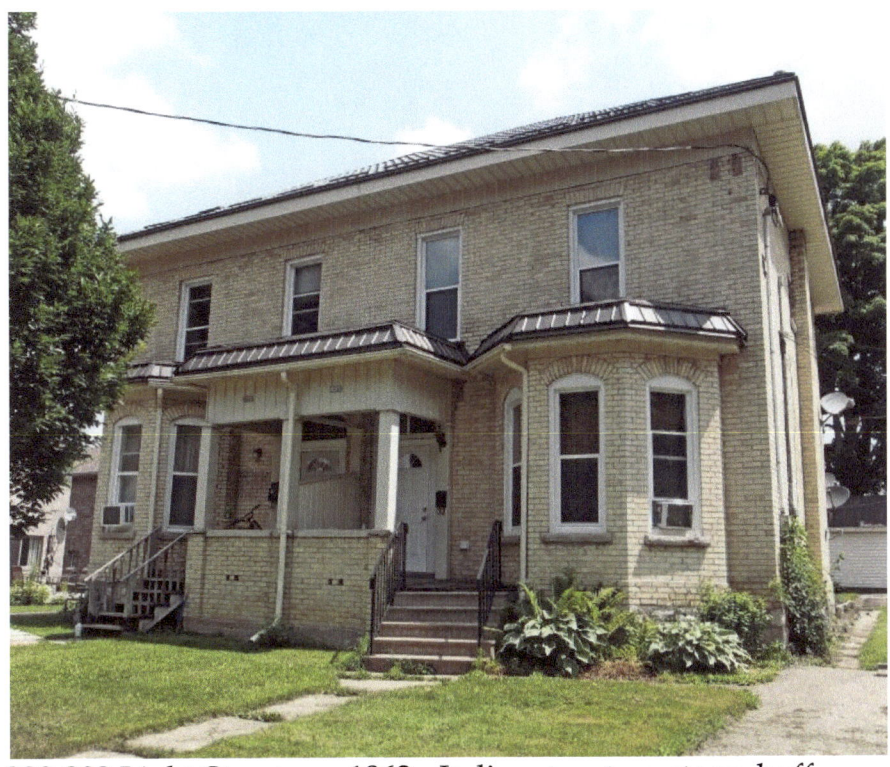

200-202 Light Street – c. 1862 - Italianate – two story, buff brick, hip roof, one-over-one ellipse shape windows on first floor, one-over-one rectangular windows on second floor, one-story bay window, porch has squared posts, door has ellipse shape transom

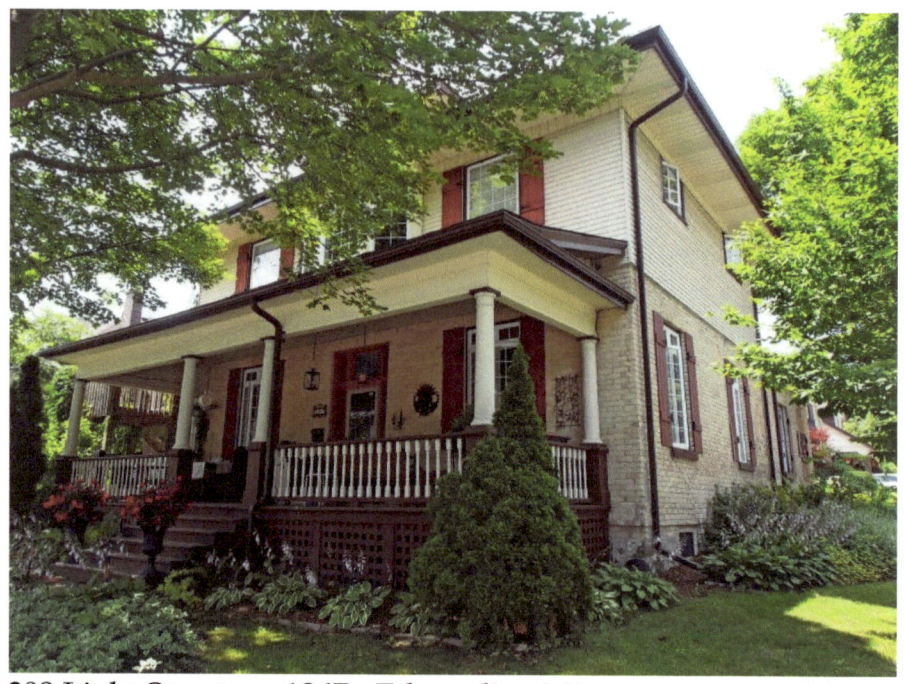

209 Light Street - c. 1867 - Edwardian Mix – two story with attic, symmetrical, painted brick and aluminum clad second floor, hip roof, deep eaves, oriel window above front door, large verandah with Doric pillars, centered door with transom and side lights

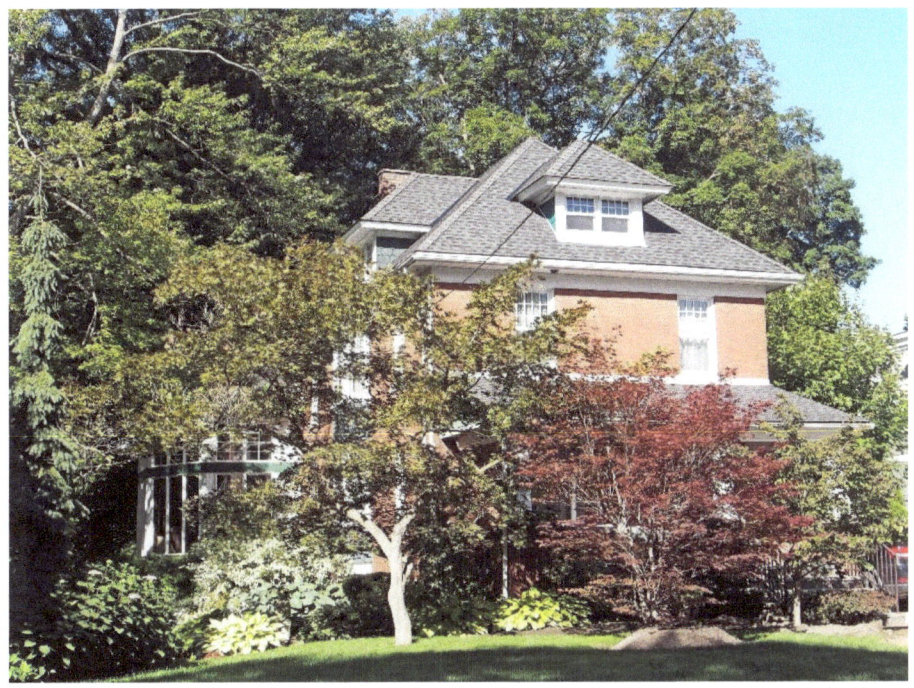

241 Light Street – c. 1884 - Edwardian style, two story with finished attic, red brick, topped hip roof, two-story bay window with painted green shingle below each set of windows, shed roof open verandah with tapered post on brick piers

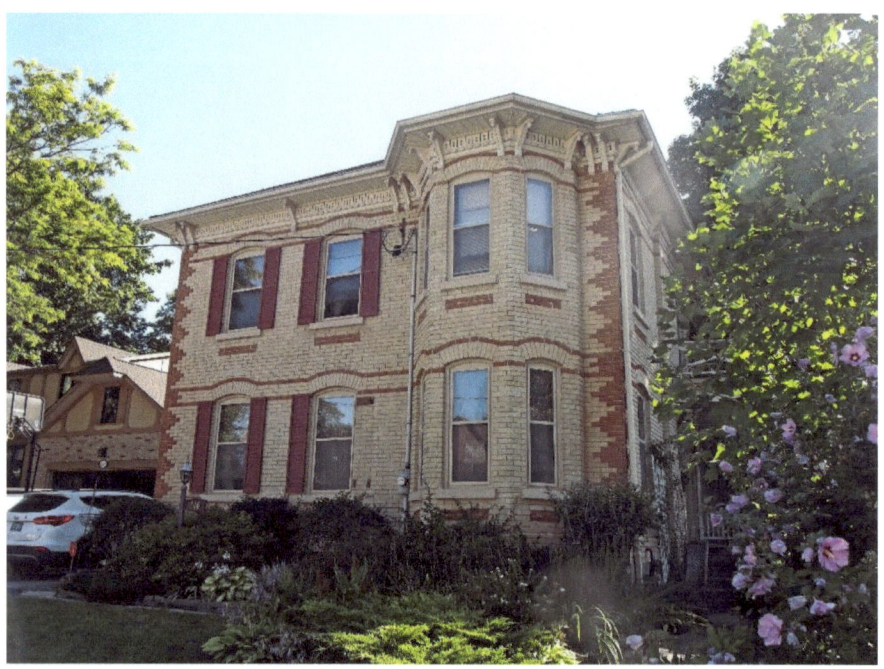

246 Light Street – c. 1877 - Italianate - two story, buff brick with red brick decorated quoins and string course, hip roof with single and paired brackets and dentils, segmental arch windows with decorated shutters, two-story bay window, porch with turned posts supports balcony, door has ellipse shape transom

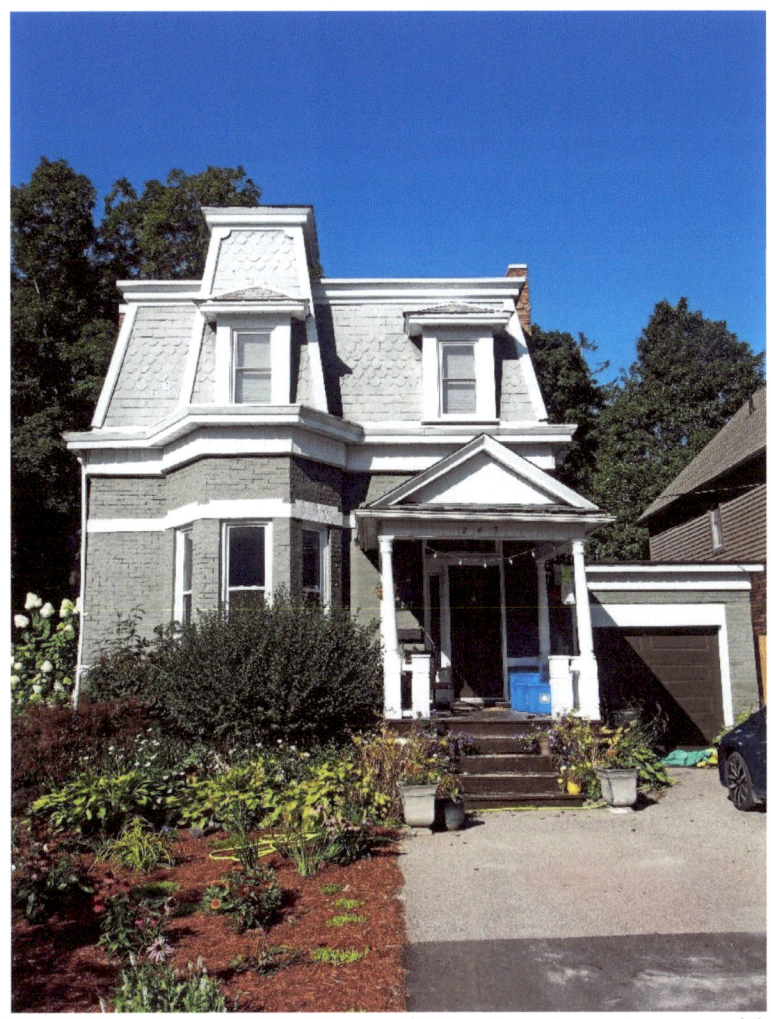

247 Light Street - c. 1884 - Second Empire, two story, red brick (painted), decorated painted wood shingles on Mansard roof, brick string course and recessed bricking beneath 1st story bay window, double front door with transom is protected by new porch, cut field stone foundation

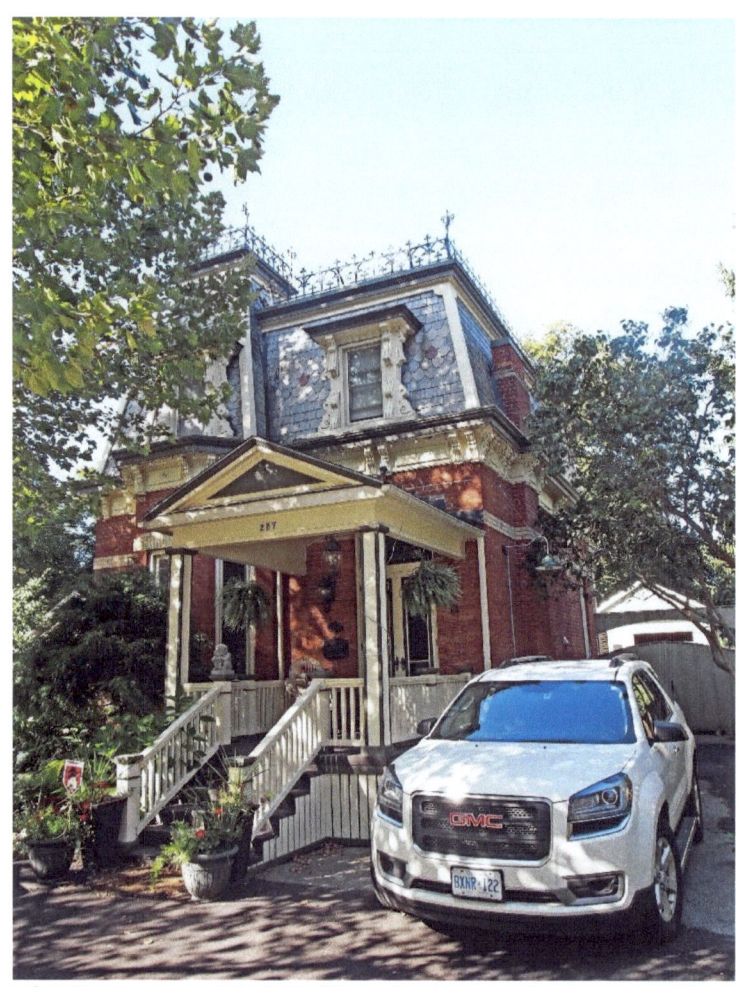

257 Light Street – c. 1860-1880 – designated - Second Empire, mansard roof, ornate dormers and iron cresting - The mansard roof was first used in France to allow more living space for bedrooms (dormers) on the top floor. It is a two-story brick house with white string course and decorated white brick beneath 1st store bay window, painted slate on Mansard roof, cresting along roof line, painted brackets, dormers are enhanced with decorative wood trim, open side porch with Doric post and brackets hint to the original design of front porch, double doors with transom, limestone foundation

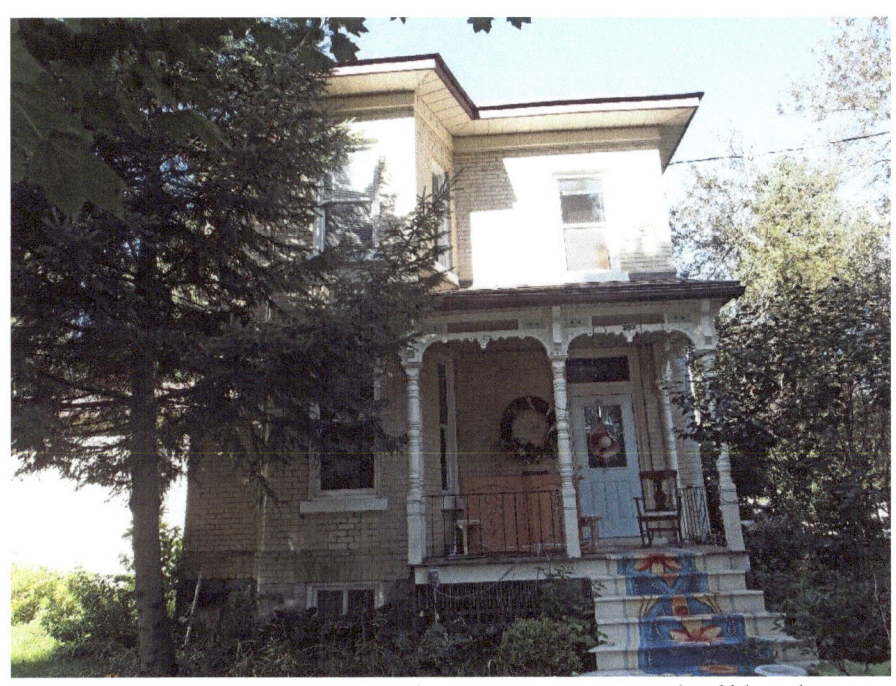

263 Light Street - c. 1868 - Italianate, two story, buff brick, decorative soldier bricking beneath second floor bay window, hip roof, door with transom is protected by porch supported by turned posts and decorative cornice, cut field stone foundation

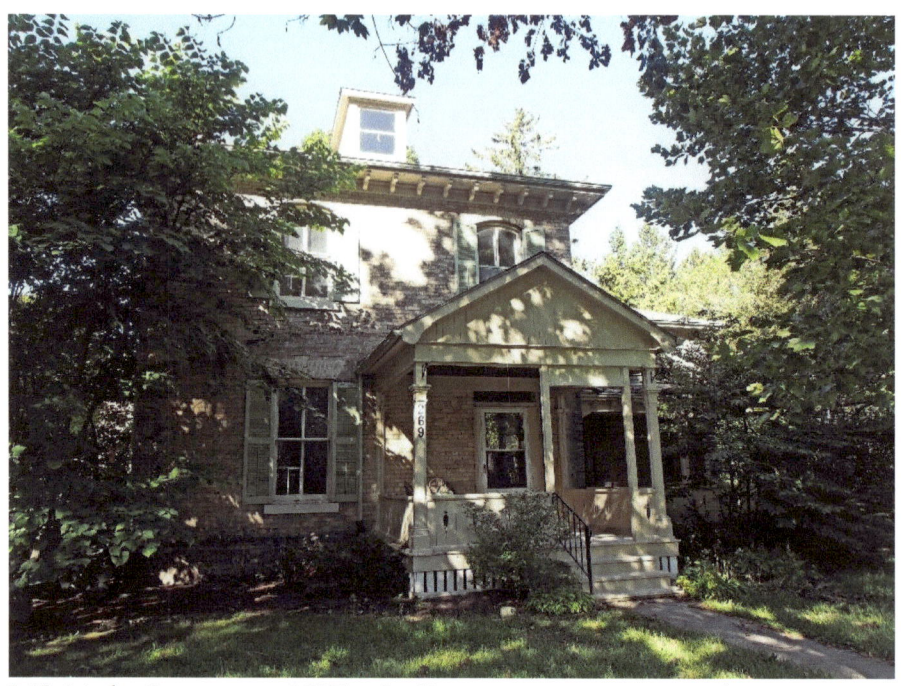

269 Light Street - c. 1875 – Italianate, two story with attic, white brick, hip roof, deep eaves with single brackets, east dormer, two-story bay window, door with transom is protected by new screened porch

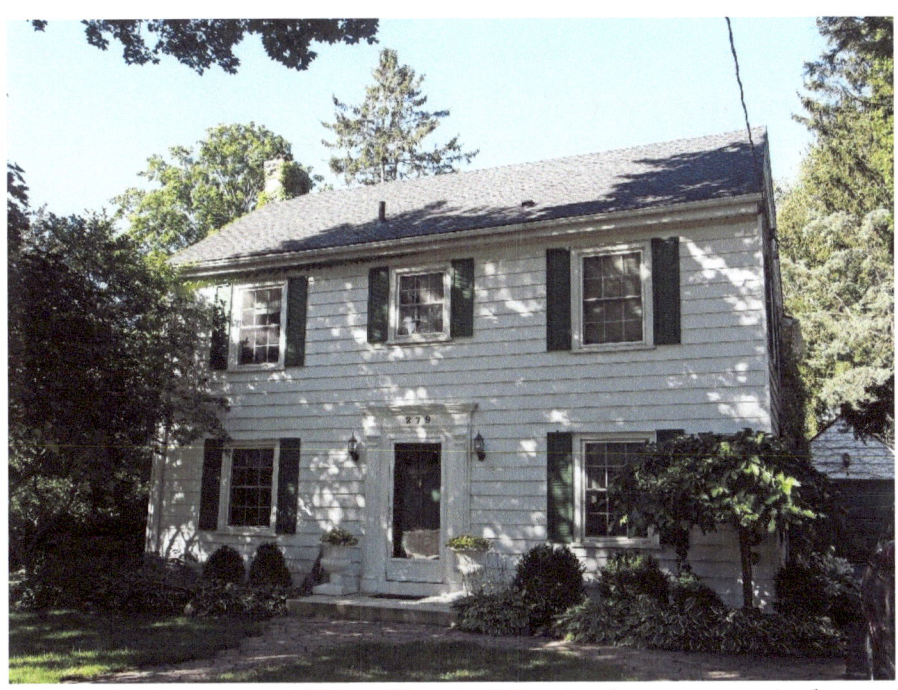

279 Light Street - c. 1878 - Classical Revival - symmetrical two story, white wood siding, gable roof, centered door is flanked with Doric pilasters supporting a thin projecting cornice

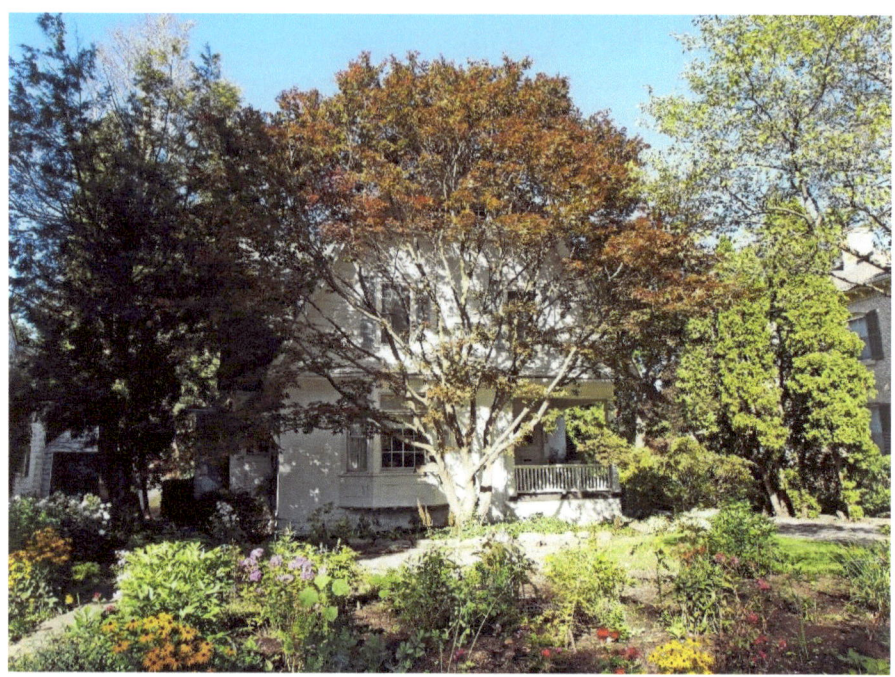
285 Light Street - c. 1880 - Modern Dutch Revival - two story with attic, white wood siding, double gambrel roof, paired 16 pane attic window, sixteen-over-one rectangular windows with decorative shutters, transom above door is protected by open porch and is contained within roof line

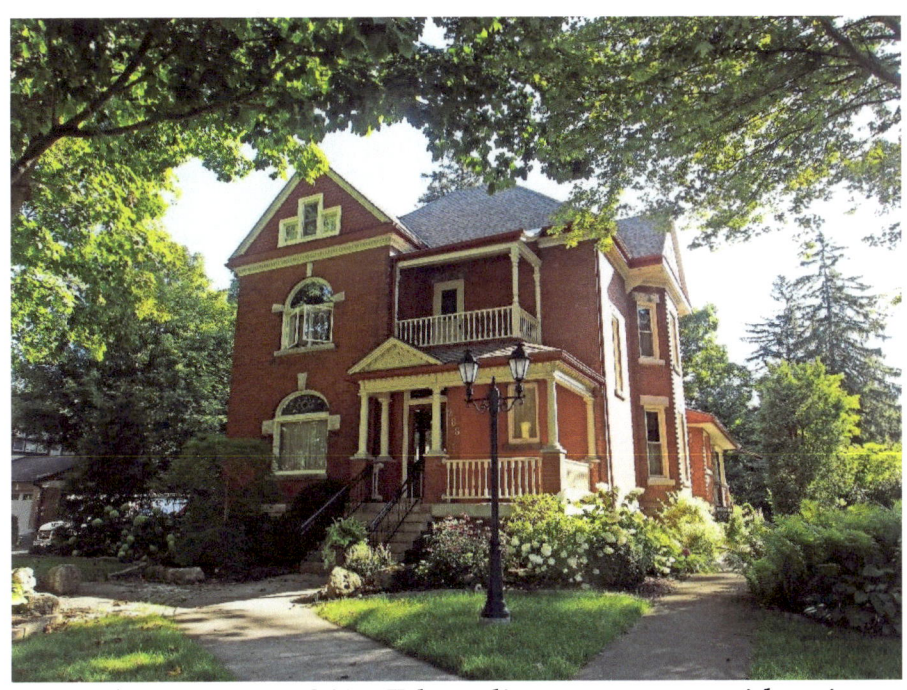

288 Light Street - c. 1861 – Edwardian - two story with attic, red brick, hip roof with gable roof over second story bay window and front extension, painted red wood shingles in gable end with Palladian windows, delicate dentils at roof and porch cornice, two large rectangular windows are topped with beautiful semi-circular stained glass windows, all windows have stone sills and keystone arched brick to match semi-circular windows, tapered Doric pillars support open porch with a small balcony which has turned posts with turned balusters, cut stone foundation

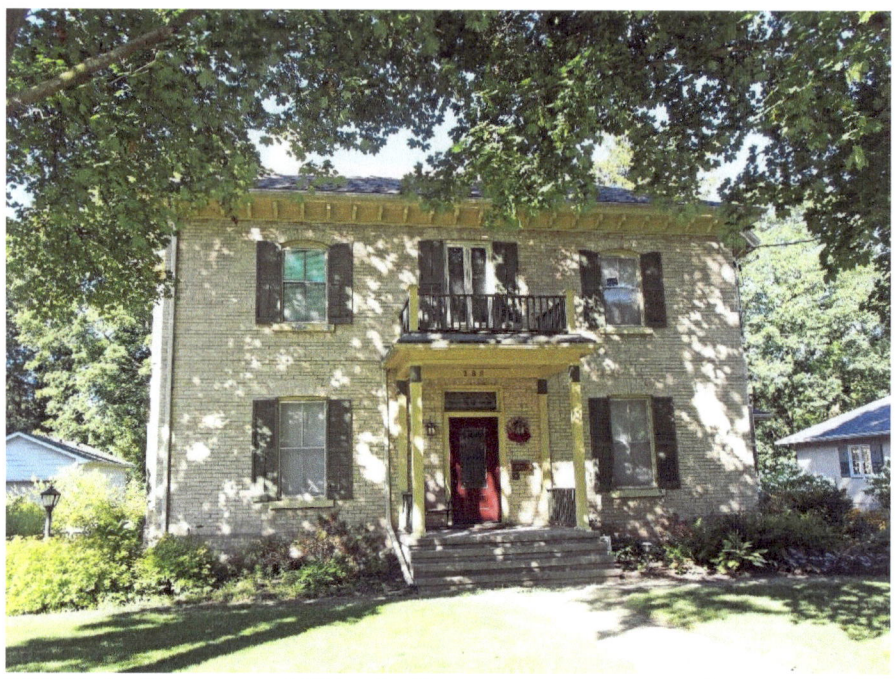

289 Light Street - c. 1851 – Italianate - symmetrical two story, white brick, hip roof, deep eaves, single brackets, rectangular two-over-two double hung windows on first floor with segmental arched windows on second floor, shutters on all windows, two story bay window with decorative soldier bricking between floors, transom above centered door, new open porch and balcony, cut field stone foundation

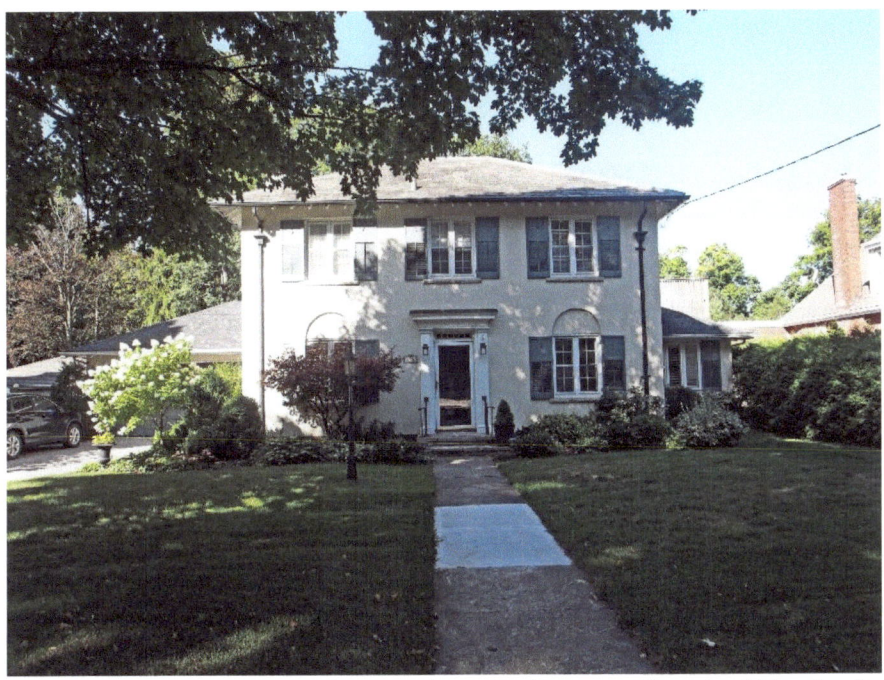

295 Light Street - c. 1880 - Modern Italianate Classical Revival style, symmetrical two story, grey smooth stucco, hip roof with exposed decorative rafters, three over three bays, four-over-four single hung windows are in pairs with decorative shutters, lower windows have decorative circular arch above windows, 8 paneled front centered door with transom, Doric pilasters flank doorway supporting a projecting three-part cornice

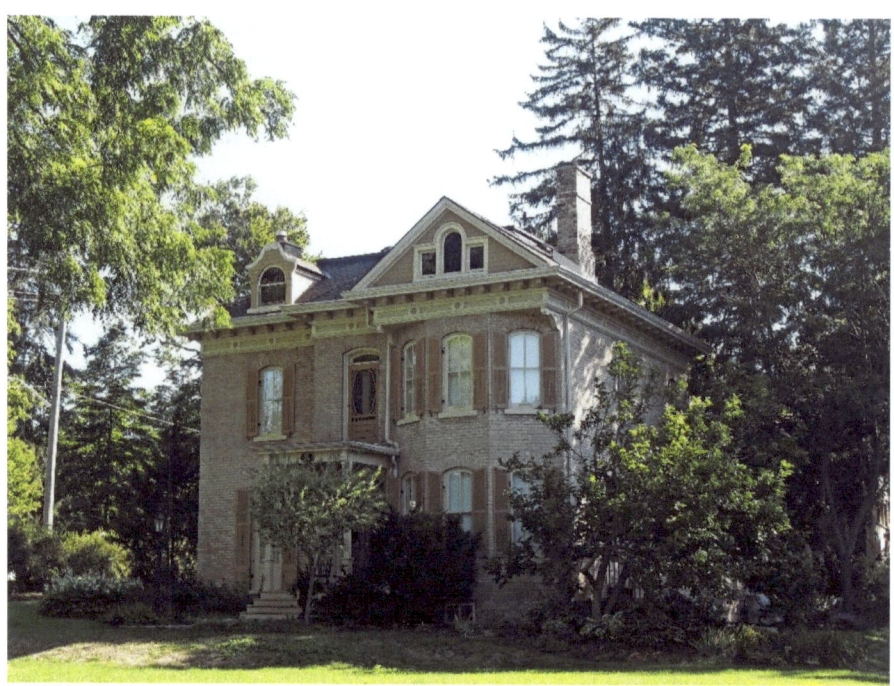

312 Light Street - c. 1881 - Italianate, two story with attic, buff brick, hip roof, fish scale painted green shingles on gable and has a Palladian window, dormer with semi-circular window, roof line with decorated cornice with single brackets, two-over-two segmental arch windows with original shutters, large open verandah extends along two sides of the house, large two-story bay window has supported brackets for a rectangular pediment roof, double door has transom

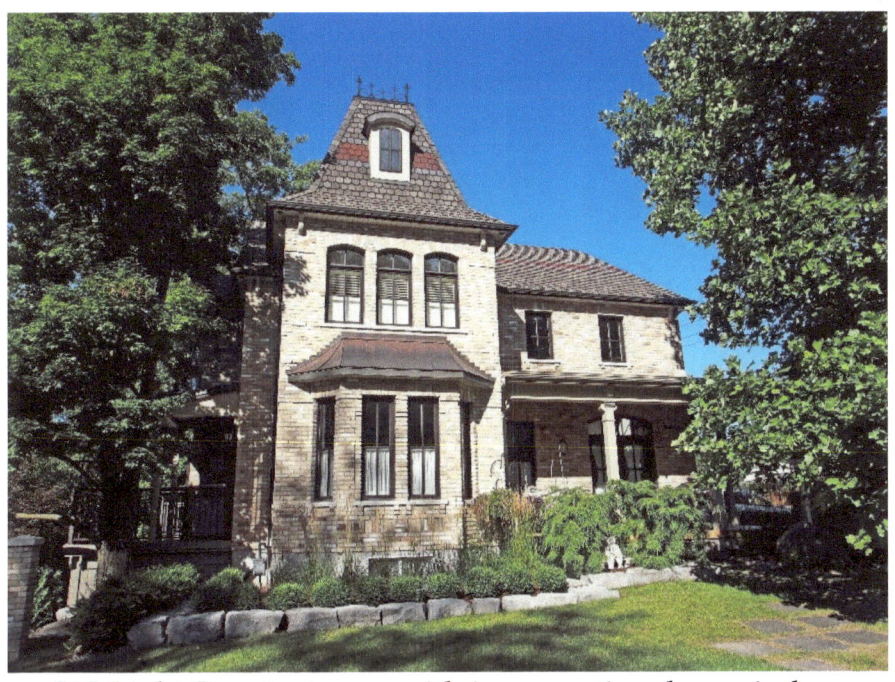

313 Light Street – tower with iron cresting, bay window

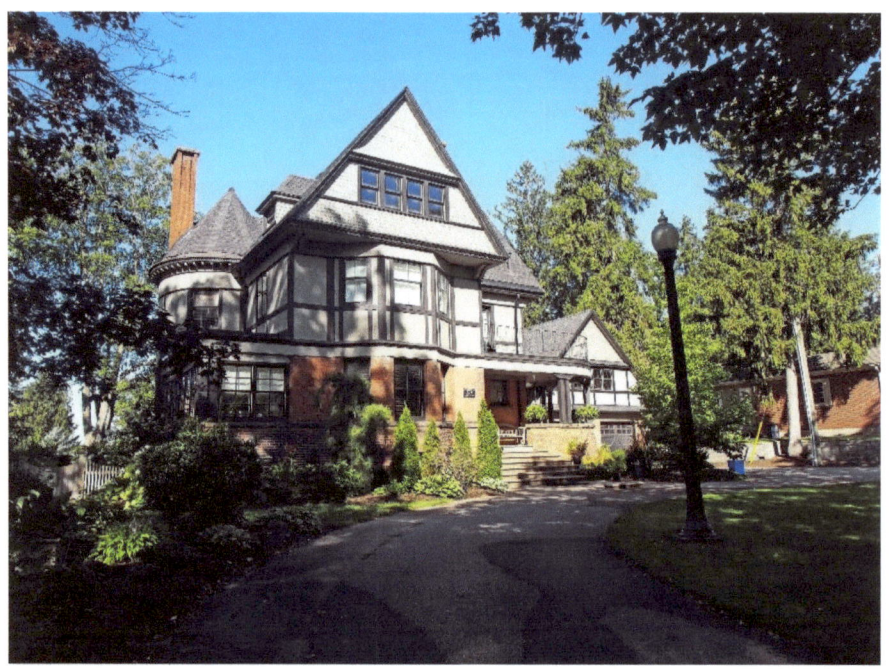

329 Light Street - c. 1890 – designated - Queen Anne, Tudor Revival styles - The residence was built circa 1890, and was formerly the residence of Andrew Pattullo and Robert Fulton. The property was given the name Gowanbank. Two story with attic, red brick with stucco/timber second floor, steep gable slate roof, deep eaves with paired brackets at corners, red sandstone circles the house separating rug brick on lower half and red brick above, an open front porch supports a balcony, round tower with cone roof and second story bay window, round verandah

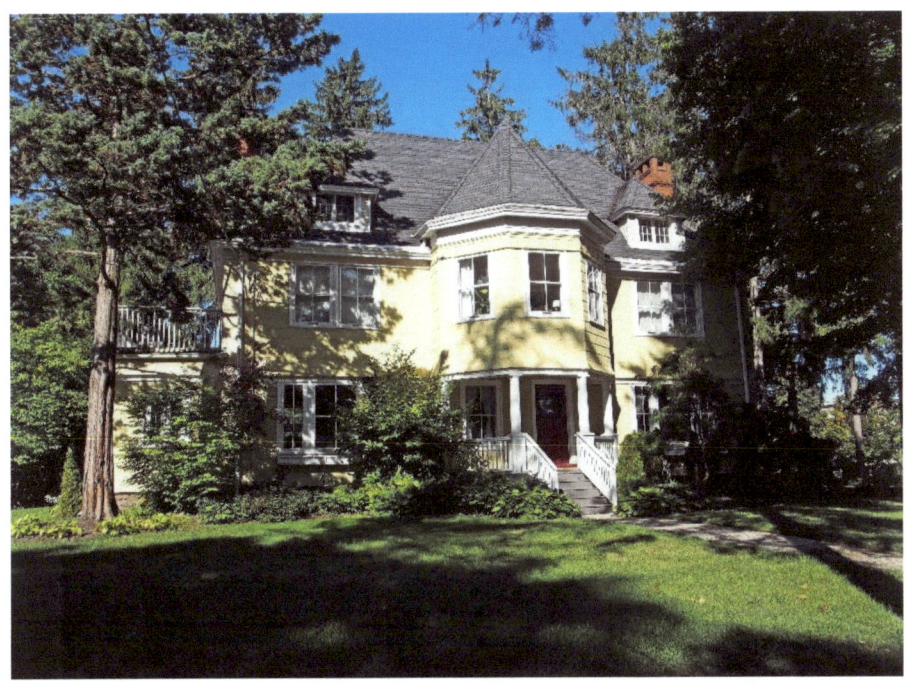

347 Light Street - c. 1895 - Queen Anne, symmetrical two story, white asbestos clad, steep, topped hip roof, with decorative cornice, rectangular two-over-two double hung windows, windows are grouped, an open front porch supports a large oriel window and protects centered door

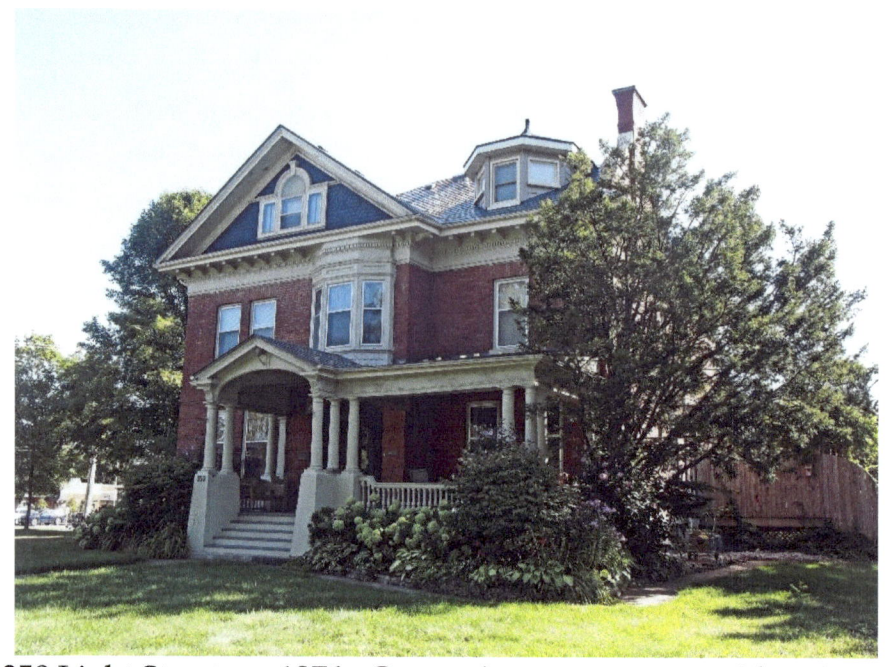

350 Light Street - c. 1876 - Queen Anne, two story with attic, red brick, front gable has painted red shingles and Palladian window, parapet chimney on south side, hip roof, deep cornice with dentils, scotch dome on west side of roof, large oriel window above front door, one-over-one double hung rectangular windows are grouped in pairs, large open verandah which also covers front steps, is supported with tapered Doric columns

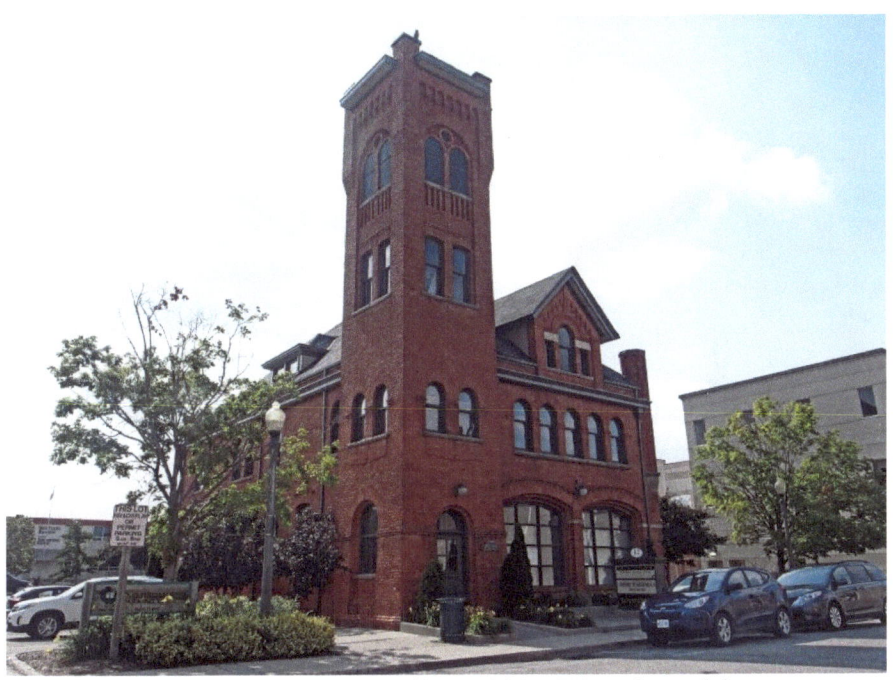

12 Perry Street – Old Fire Hall c. 1899 - Woodstock's municipal Fire Department's history begins with the installation of fire hydrants in 1881. Access to water under pressure requires professional fire fighters. Horses pulled the fire engines well into the 20th century. Motorized fire engines were built by the R.S. Bickle Company beginning in 1900.

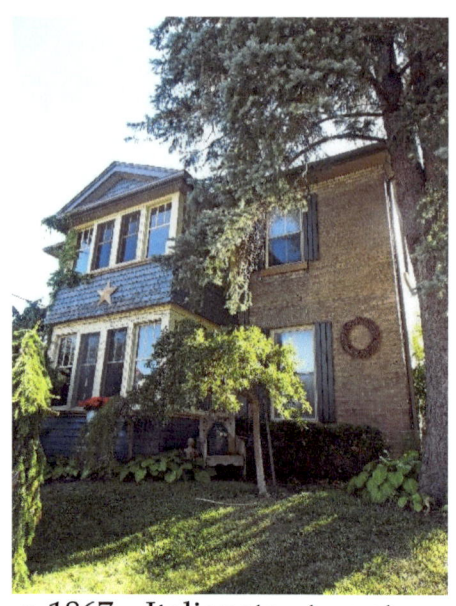

69 Perry Street - c. 1867 – Italianate - two story, yellow brick, hip roof, two-over-two rectangular windows, front gable closed porch and balcony, with shingle skirt

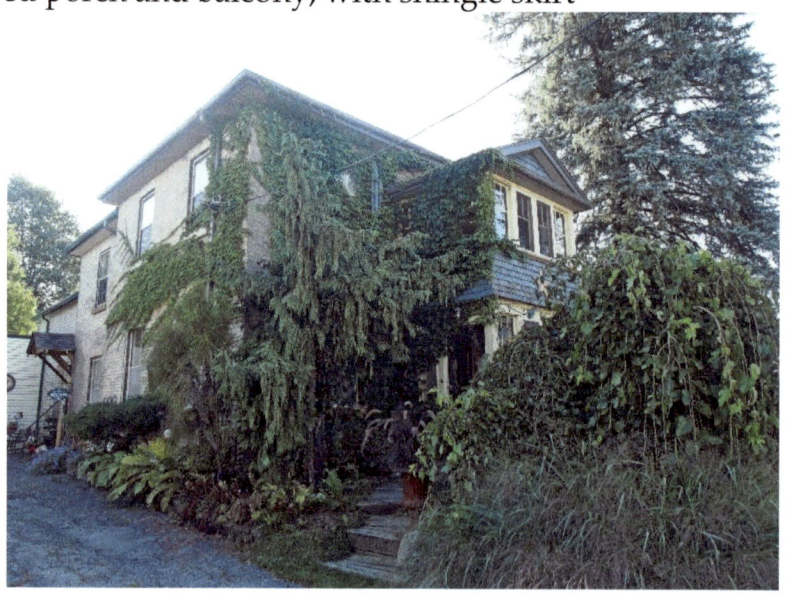

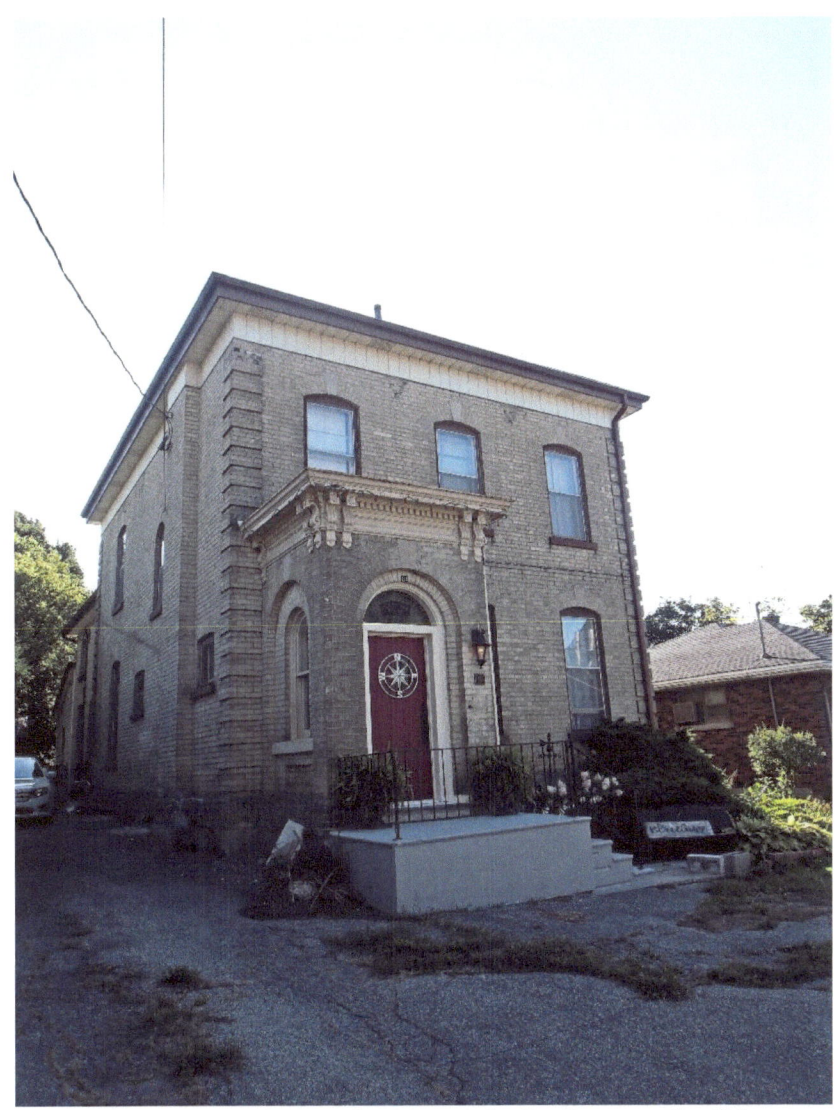

81 Perry Street - c. 1875 – designated - Italianate, builder was William Thompson - two story, yellow brick, quoins, trunked hip roof, flat roof closed porch, with decorative paired bracket with semi-circular one-over-one windows, cement platform porch with aluminum railing

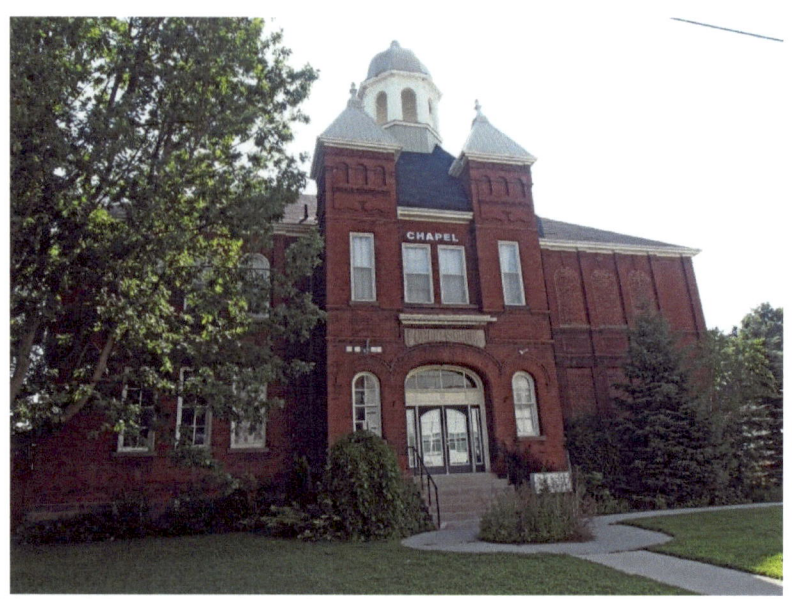

27 Chapel Street – Chapel Public School – twin towers flank the entrance, cupola on roof top

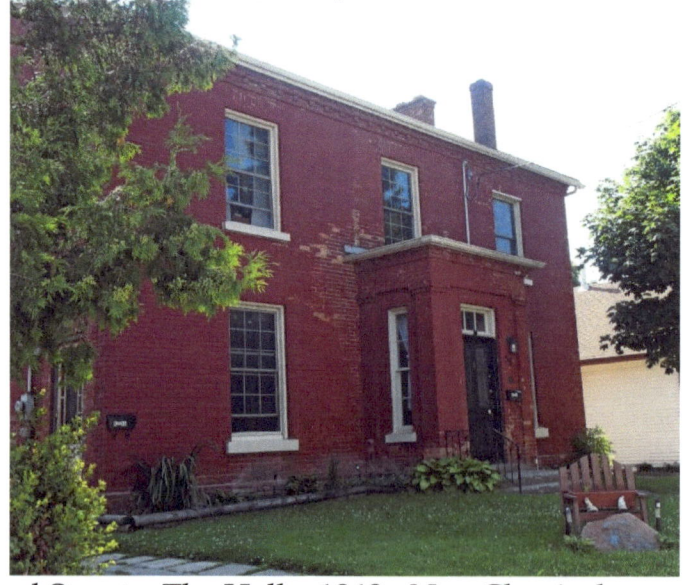

55 Chapel Street – The Hall – 1848 - Neo-Classical - two story, symmetrical, painted brick, side gable roof, decorative brick cornice, three-light transom

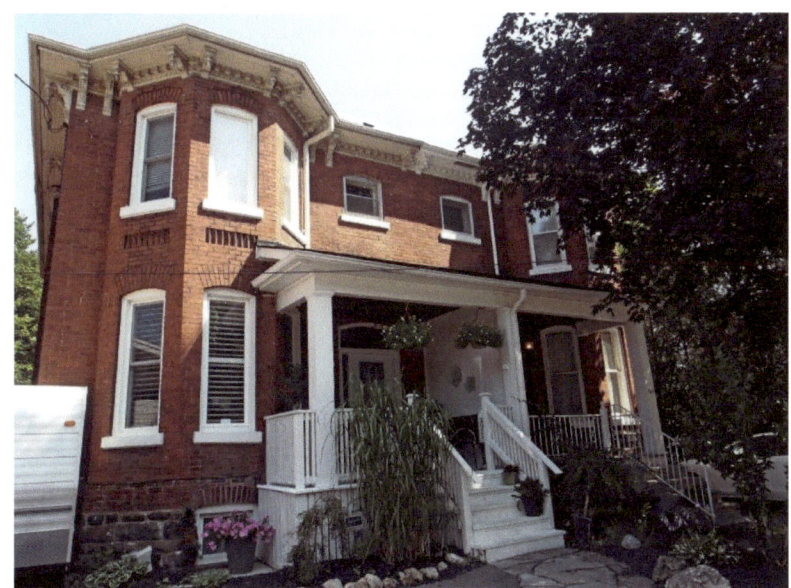

565 Simcoe Street – Italianate, cornice brackets and dentil moulding, saw tooth decorative brickwork, two-storey bays

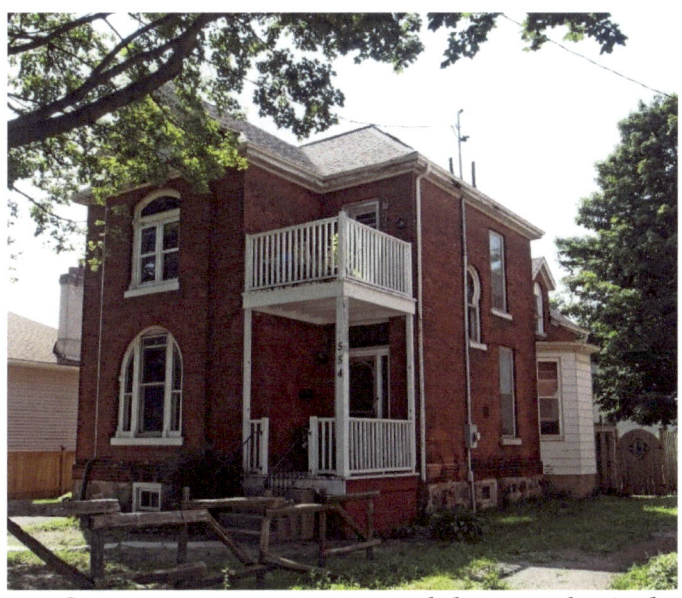

554 Simcoe Street – two storey verandah, round windows, keyhole window on side

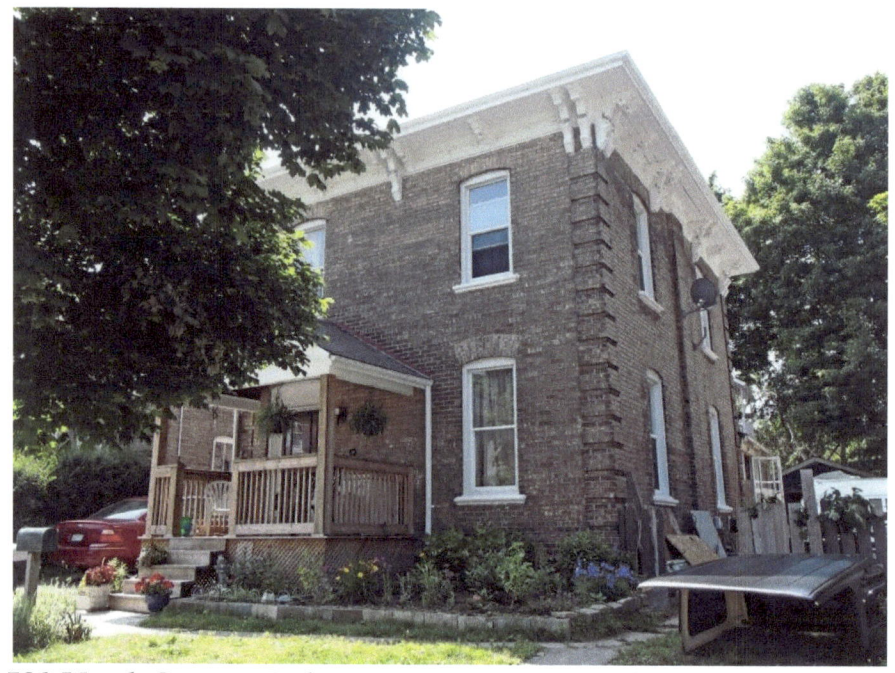

590 Hatch Street – Italianate - two story, buff brick with decorative quoins, hip roof, decorative cornice, brackets in pairs, field stone foundation

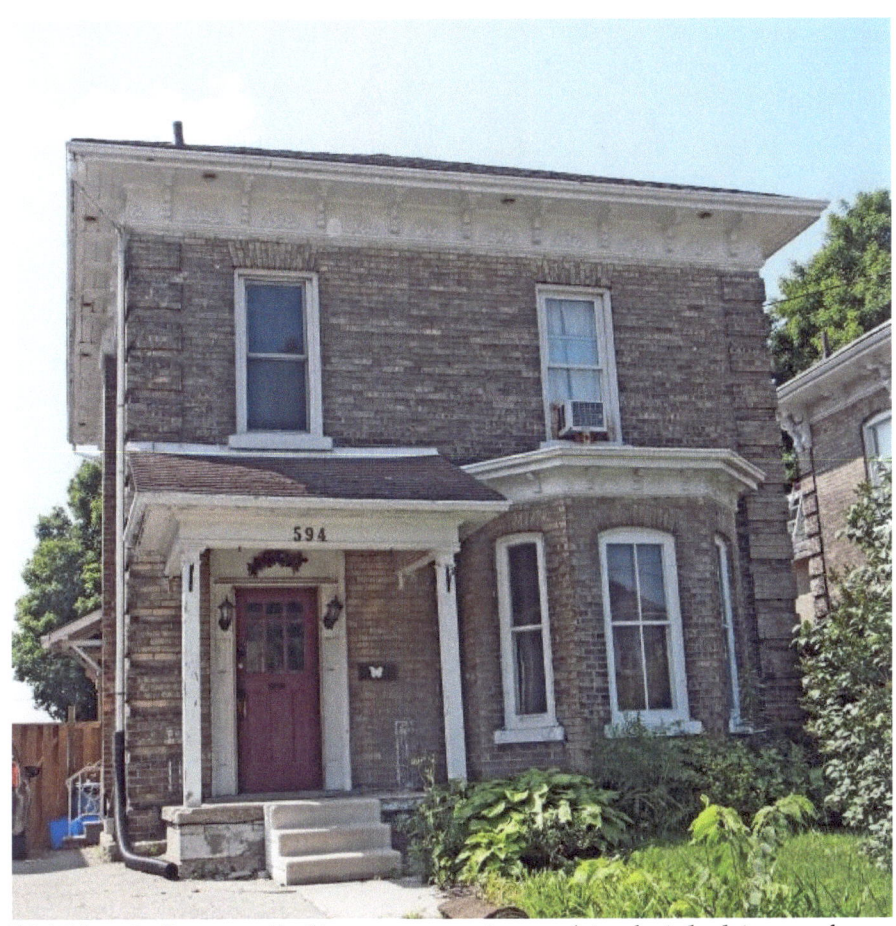

594 Hatch Street – Italianate - quoins, white brick, hip roof, first story bay window, decorative cornice, single brackets repeated on bay window, Doric piers support shed roof porch

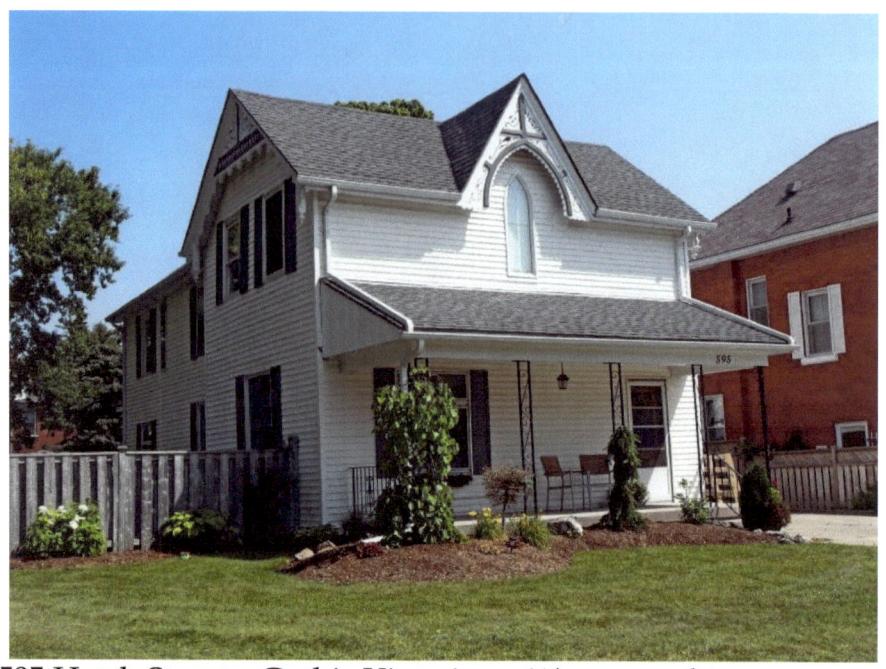

595 Hatch Street – Gothic Victorian - 1½ story, white clapboard, gable roof with delicate vergeboard, pendant posts at corners, front Gothic window

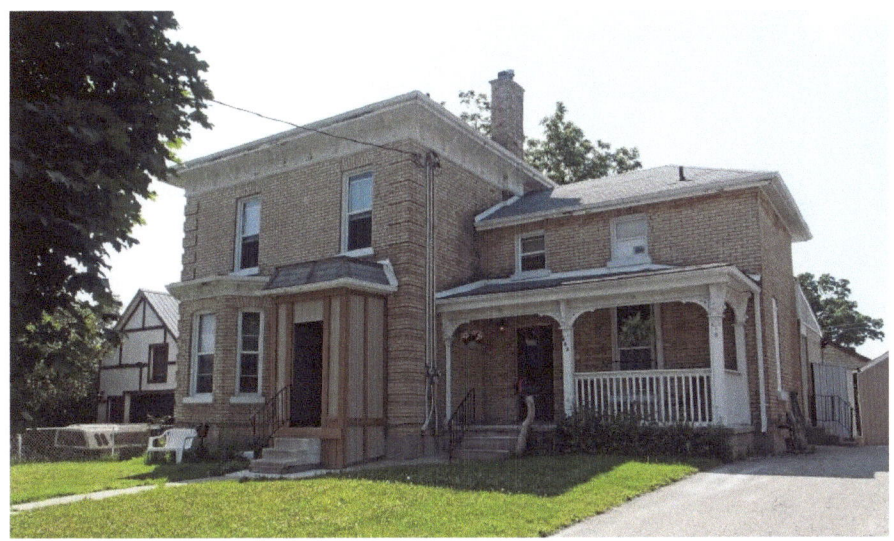

602 Hatch Street - – Italianate - L shape two story, white brick, decorative quoins, hip roof, single brackets and decorative cornice, one-story flat roof bay window with cornice and bracket design repeated, decorative storm door with mansard roof, side verandah has turned posts and brackets

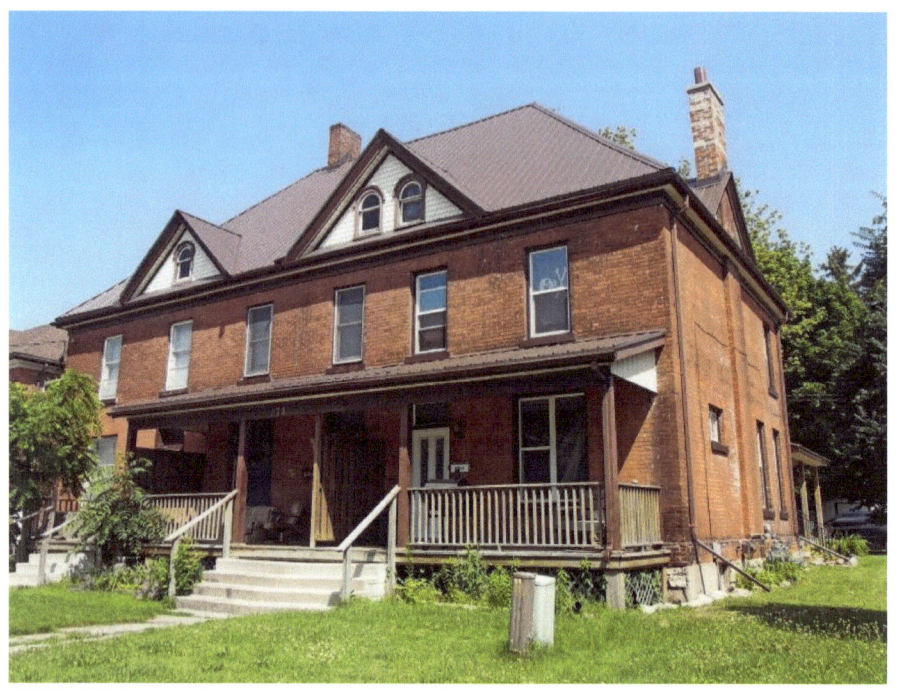

#571-575 Hatch Street - Edwardian Town Houses - two story, red brick, steep hip roof with gable dormer, semi-circular and rectangular windows, rectangular transoms

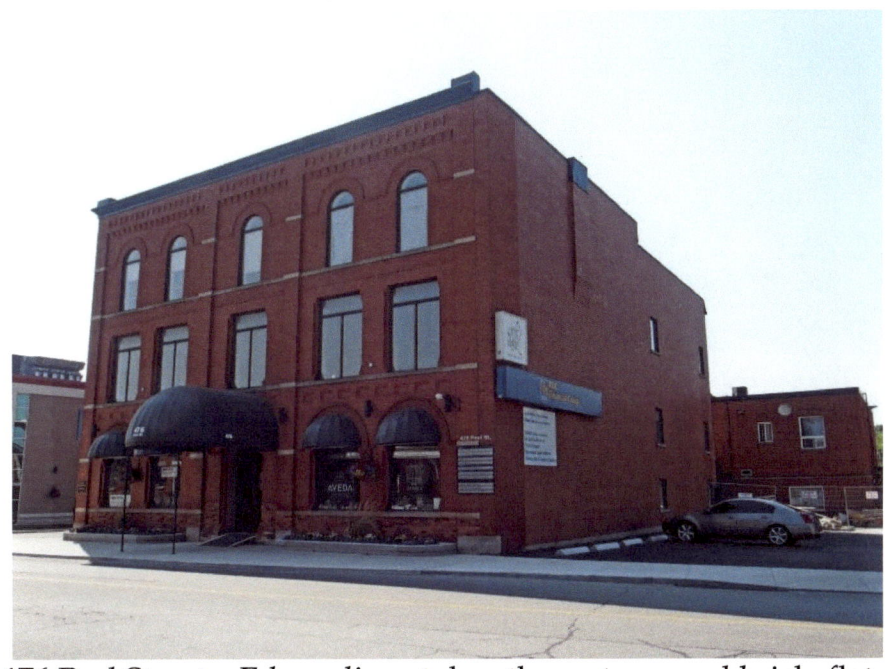

476 Peel Street – Edwardian style – three storey red brick, flat roof – decorative brickwork, patterned cornice, drip mouldings above the windows

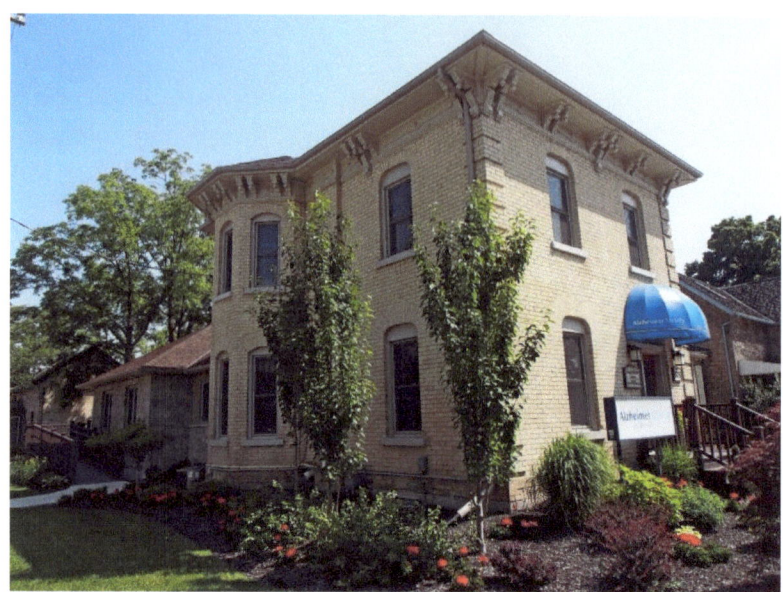

575 Peel Street – c. 1874 - Italianate – L shape two story, buff brick with decorative quoins, hip roof with gable roof on side addition, paired brackets on decorative cornice, two-story bay window

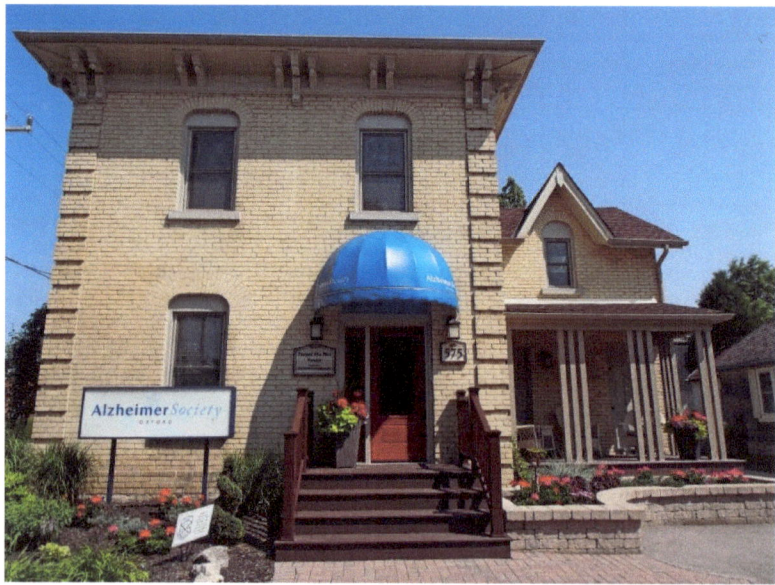

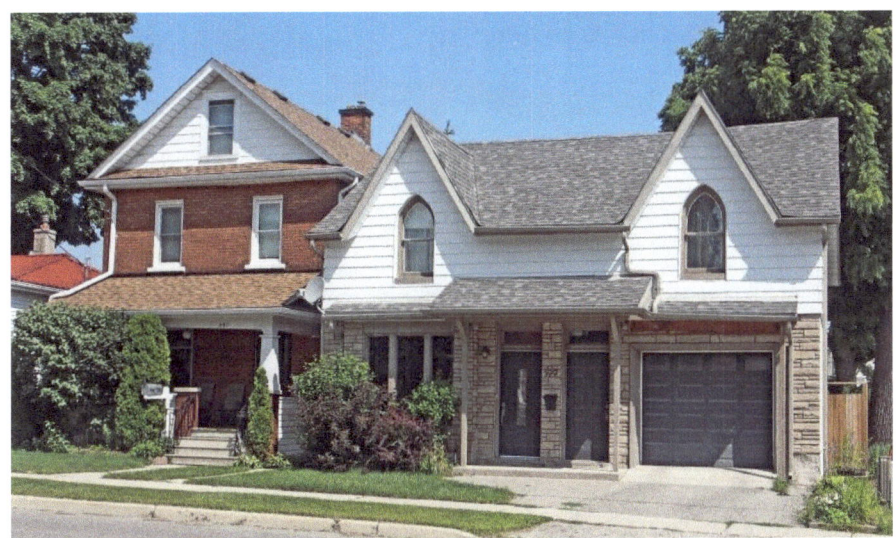

597 Peel Street – c. 1853 – Edwardian - two story, red brick, gable roof, aluminum siding in gable end, verandah has tapered wood rectangular piers on brick pedestals

599 Peel Street – separate newer house with round-headed windows in gables

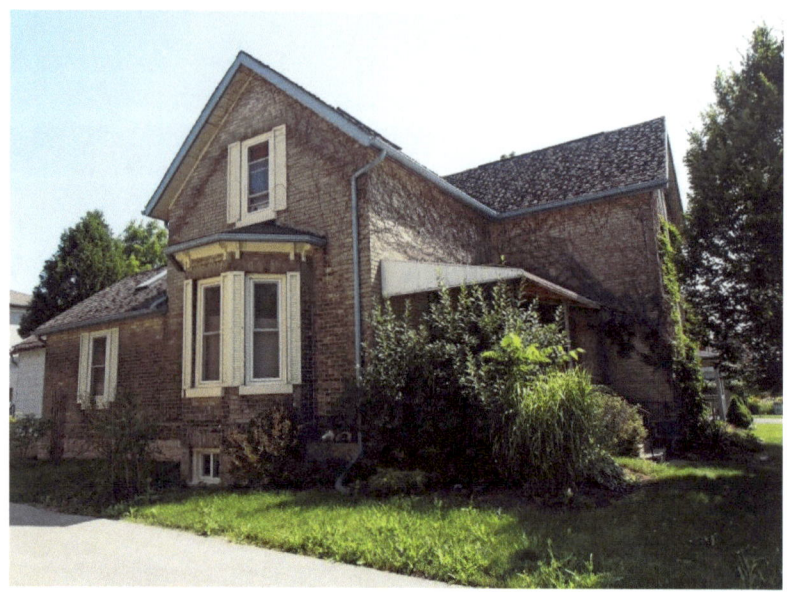

581 Peel Street – c. 1875 - Ontario Vernacular - 1½ story, L shape, buff brick, front and side gable roof, decorative vergeboard in gable ends, one-story bay window with decorative brackets

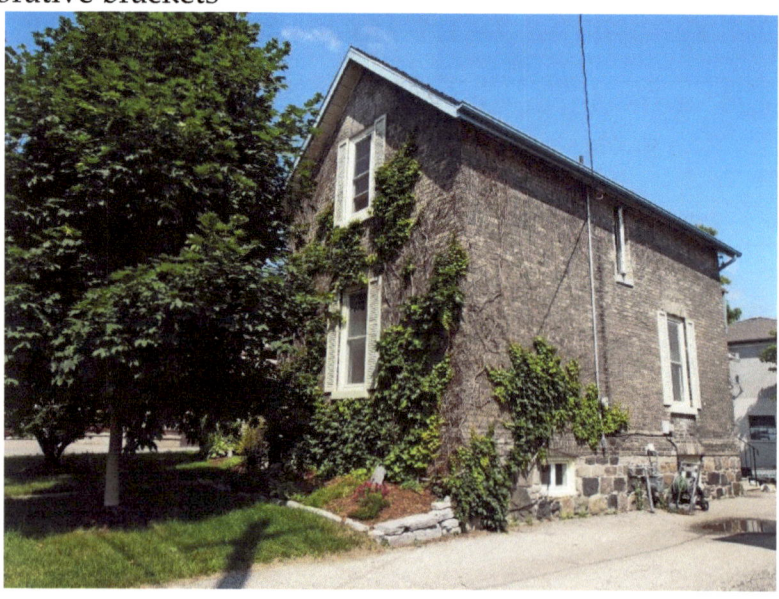

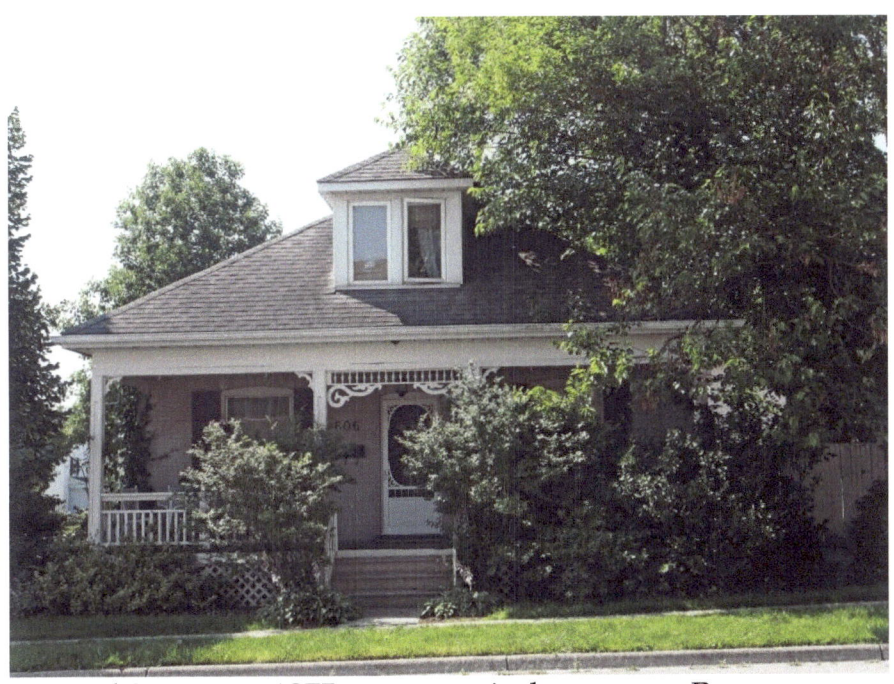

606 Peel Street – c. 1875 - symmetrical one-story Regency cottage with finished attic, red brick now painted, trunked hip roof, front hip dormer, continuance of roof forms roof of verandah

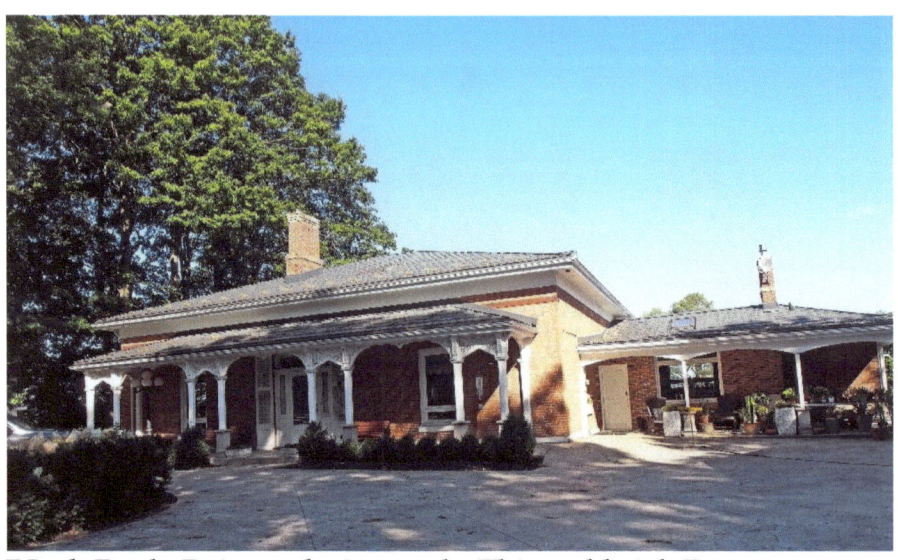

7 Jack Poole Drive – designated - This red brick Regency Cottage was built by Honorable George Alexander who was member for Oxford. Later, he became Oxford's first Senator, being appointed by Sir John A. MacDonald. The house, built in 1857 by D. M. McKay, appears to have been constructed on an earlier foundation. It has been beautifully restored. Senator Alexander's daughter, Isabella Maude, married John Pennefather Vansittart, the eldest son of John George Vansittart of Bysham Park. Although named Rokewood, it was once known as Fair Villa as the house faced south overlooking the old Fairgrounds property. In 1806, the Prince of Whales, later Edward VIII, was entertained here.

## Architectural Terms

| | |
|---|---|
| Capital: The uppermost finish or decoration on a column. A Doric column is characterized by a plain column with no base, a shaft with twenty flutings, and a simple capital with a simple entablature.<br>Example: 39 Light Street, Page 6 | |
| **Cupola:** A domed or curved roof rising from a building as a decorative element.<br><br>Example: 27 Chapel Street, Page 47 | |
| **Iron Cresting**: A decorative ornament along the top of a roof. Iron cresting was popular in the Baroque era and also in Italianate, Victorian, Second Empire and Queen Anne styles of architecture.<br>Example: 139 Light Street, Page 41 | |
| Mansard Roof: This style was popularized by Francois Mansart (1598-1666), an accomplished architect of the French Baroque period and especially fashionable during the Second French Empire (1852-1870). This roof is almost flat on the top section, with two slopes on each of its sides with the lower slope at a steeper angle than the upper and having dormer windows.<br>Example: 51 Light Street, Page 46 | |
| Window Hood: A hood is the piece found above window openings, usually of an ornate design, and covers the top third of the opening. Hoods are commonly placed above arched or curved openings on both windows and doors.<br>Example: 57 Light Street, Page 59 | |

Building Styles

| | |
|---|---|
| **Classical Revival,** 1820-1860 – This style was an analytical, scientific, and dogmatic revival based on intensive studies of Greek and Roman buildings, concerned with the application of Greek plans and proportions to civic buildings. Schools, libraries, government offices, and most other civic buildings were built in the Classical Revival style. The white columned porches of the Classical Revival domestic buildings are identified with the mansions of wealthy land owners in Canada.<br>Example: 279 Light Street, Page | 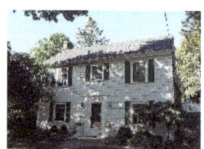 |
| **Dutch Colonial Revival**, 1890-1930 - is distinguished by its gambrel roof, with or without flared eaves, and the frequent use of dormers. The gambrel style allowed an almost complete second floor without the expense of two-story construction. Characteristics: 1½ to 2 storeys, clapboard or shingle siding, usually symmetrical facades, gable-end chimneys, round windows in gable end, porch under overhanging eaves, shed, hipped or gable dormers, columns for porches and entry.<br>Example: 285 Light Street, Page 36 | 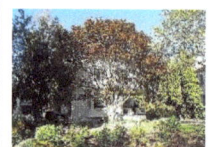 |

| | |
|---|---|
| Gothic Revival, 1830-1890 – These decorative buildings have sharply-pitched gables with highly detailed verge boards, pointed-arch window openings, and dichromatic brickwork. It is a common style in Ontario. Example: 81 Light Street, Page 57 | 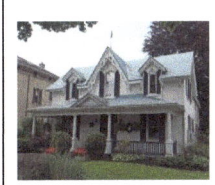 |
| **Italianate**, 1850-1900 – A two story rectangular building with a mild hip roof, a projecting frontispiece, and generous eaves with ornate cornice brackets was the basis of the style; often there are large sash windows, quoins, ornate detailing on the windows, belvederes and wraparound verandahs. Italianate commercial buildings often have cast iron cresting and elegant window surrounds. Example: 77 Light Street, Page 8 | 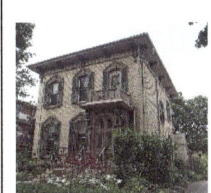 |
| Neo-Classical (1810 - 1850) – This style was a direct result of the War of 1812. Many Upper Canadians returning from the war with the United States were second or third generation Loyalists who had inherited land and means from their forefathers. Once the conflict had passed, they had the money and the time to expand their holdings and indulge their architectural whims. Both residential and commercial buildings were constructed on the traditional Georgian plan, but they had a new gaiety and light-heartedness. Detailing became more refined, delicate, and elegant. Example: 147 Light Street, Page 51 | 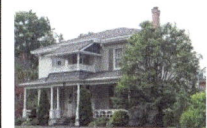 |

| | |
|---|---|
| Queen Anne, 1885-1900 – This style is distinguished by an irregular outline featuring a combination of an offset tower, broad gables, projecting two-storey bays, verandahs, multi-sloped roofs, and tall, decorative chimneys. A mixture of brick and wood is common. Windows often have one large single-paned bottom sash and small panes in the upper sash.<br>Example: 33 Light Street, Page 61 | |
| Second Empire, 1860-1880 – The mansard roof is the most noteworthy feature of this style and is evidence of the French origins. Projecting central towers and one or two-storey bays can also be present.<br>Example: 57 Light Street, Page 59 | |
| Tudor Revival – exposed timbers with stucco infill, multi-paned windows.<br><br>Example: 93 Light Street | |

# Other Books by Barbara Raue

Coins of Gold
Arrows, Indians and Love
The Life and Times of Barbara
The Cromwell Family Book
Laura Secord Discovered
Daddy Where Are You?

Montana Series
Book 1: Montana Dream
Book 2: Life on the Montana Frontier
Book 3: Montana to Boston and Back
Book 4: Montana Sons Go to War
Book 5: Montana Sons Return from War

Book 1: Rite of Passage
Book 2: Rite of Marriage

© 2019 by Barbara Raue - All the photos in this book have been taken with my cameras. I own the rights to them.

www.ingramcontent.com/pod-product-compliance
Lightning Source LLC
Chambersburg PA
CBHW040236220526
45473CB00001B/261